Designer Dogs

Designer Dogs

The definitive guide to finding
the right designer dog for you

Interpet Publishing

First published in UK by
Interpet Publishing
Vincent Lane,
Dorking,
Surrey,
RH4 3YX

Produced by Millennium House Pty Ltd
52 Bolwarra Rd, Elanora Heights, NSW, 2101, Australia
Ph: 612 9970 6850
Fax: 612 9970 8136
email rightsmanager@millenniumhouse.com.au

ISBN 13: 978 1 84286 139 4
ISBN 10: 1 84286 139 5

Millennium House would like to hear from photographers interested in supplying photographs

Printed in China

Cover photograph by Kathy Young, back cover photograph by Melinda Radus
Cover design by Alex Frampton
Publisher: Gordon Cheers
Associate Publisher: Margaret Olds
Project Manager and Editor: Catherine Etteridge
Text: Norma Bennett Woolf; consultant veterinarian Dr. Matthew Miles (BVSc, MRCVS); crossbred profiles compiled by Catherine Etteridge; "Choosing a reputable breeder" by Kathy Young; "Caring for your puppy" by Melinda Radus
Advisers: Professor Frank Nicholas (BScAgr, PhD), Melinda Radus, Kate Schoeffel (BSc (Hons), BVSc), Sonja Walsh
Designer: Alex Frampton
Picture research: Catherine Etteridge
Index: Glenda Browne
Photographs: James Young, Melinda Radus, Kathy Young, Guide Dogs Victoria, Guide Dogs Queensland, Marg Laughlin, Michael Barry, Carole Schatz, Amy Lane, Malinda DeVincenzi, Jack Phipps, Shannon Woodrow, David Wolfe, Robin Cahill, Lynda Kadziorski, Mary Jane Kovacs, Kristine Robards, Tracy Pozayt, Laura Fenton, Daryl Woods, Monica Capobianco, Heather Hill, Steven Scott, Bronwyn Hinder, Chelle Calbert, Sarah Levy, Carrie Allen, Linda Rogers, Sandy Wasicek, Cindy Kintzel, Penny Rangi, Kelly Teaff, Margaret Hennessy, Vanessa Jordanovich, Matthew and Sara Manuel

Contents

Introduction

By Norma Bennett Woolf

I have loved and been fascinated by dogs for most of my life, a fascination that crystallized nearly 20 years ago when I began taking a mixed-breed dog to obedience classes. For the past 15 years or so, I have owned purebreds (Akitas and Canaan Dogs), but I am intrigued by the growing number of people who seek specific crossbreds and are just as proud and pleased with their pets as those of us who believe that purebreds are the greatest.

When my children went off to college and their own lives, my fascination with dogs became a career in writing about dogs and an avocation as a dog trainer, exhibitor, and now breeder. Over the years, I have written dozens of breed profiles. Researching these profiles drove home one fact over and over—today's purebred dogs are most often the result of early combinations of breeds crossed to produce dogs of particular temperament, aptitude, size, coat type, bone structure, and skill.

Over the years, I have also become convinced that the canine-human bond is precious, regardless of the breed or mix of dog. The human relationship with dogs is not duplicated with any other animal; the dog helps with chores, shares and guards our homes, teaches us compassion and patience, and brings joy and affection into our lives. We originally became partners out of mutual need, but we each relished and expanded our roles into an association broader and more profound than an alliance for survival. That association does not depend on the dog's shape, size, coat type, or capacity to herd,

hunt, or guard; it depends on his affinity for life with a human family.

Dogs and humans have hung around together for about 12,000 years. In the beginning, dogs were probably camp followers and scavengers, and for most of canine/human history, affection and companionship took a backseat to utility. At first, dogs lived on the outskirts of settlements. Later, they hauled goods, tracked or flushed game for the table, and killed large predators that threatened nomadic people and their livestock. The development of agriculture turned wanderers into farmers, and the dog earned his keep by defending food stores from vermin, herding sheep, and protecting shepherds and their flocks. As time and civilization progressed, we took advantage of special canine characteristics and developed —perhaps at first by accident—various types of dogs to pursue particular trades in specific types of terrain or habitats, or to occupy various niches in the human environment.

Dog types varied according to their region of origin and assigned task. Farmers, shopkeepers, hunters, seamen, and others who valued and used dogs, began to refine types into breeds with specialized skills: pointers, setters, retrievers, and spaniels for hunting game birds; scenthounds for hunting rabbits and foxes; shepherds and collies for herding sheep in a variety of circumstances; working dogs to drive livestock to market; sighthounds for pursuing large, swift game in open spaces; and terriers for hunting and killing vermin. Along the way, they bred

Modern crossbreds

Today, most of the original dog careers have disappeared. Some farmers and ranchers still use dogs to herd sheep or cattle, hunters still use dogs to find game, and dogs still pull sleds in some areas. However, the vast majority of dog owners choose a dog for looks, size, ease of grooming, or other qualities and don't care about purity of lineage, conformity of appearance, or traditional skills. Instead, modern dogs—purebred, crossbred, and mixed breed—have found niches in law enforcement, as assistance and therapy dogs, as athletic competitors, and as pets. While purebred dogs excel at these tasks and working mixed breeds are rare, crossbred dogs have achieved a certain popularity, especially as service and therapy dogs and as pets.

Unlike breeders of the past who developed breeds for a particular job or set of jobs, today's responsible crossbred breeders seem to have three things in mind: producing pet dogs that don't shed much and therefore have a lower expectation of causing or exacerbating human allergic reactions; moderating the trainability or disposition of offspring by choosing parent breeds of different temperaments; and ameliorating the breathing difficulties common in short-faced (brachycephalic) dogs such as the Pekingese, Pug, and Shih Tzu. As with breeders of purebred dogs, the crossbreeders' rate of success depends on their dedication, knowledge, and experience.

There are many books on the market that help puppy buyers select the right breed for their circumstances and choose a responsible breeder as a source for a puppy. This book helps those who seek a crossbred dog follow the same procedures: look at

dogs within and across types to get the characteristics they wanted.

Those who developed the breeds we know today practiced crossbreeding only after assessing the dogs they had and deciding on attributes they wanted to add, subtract, or maintain. They concentrated on the end result they wanted to achieve and culled dogs that didn't meet their ideals. They blended instinct for the job with physical traits that made the dog a master performer. They gave weather-resistant coats to breeds that worked in harsh climates; dropears to dogs that worked in close cover; a love of people to dogs that worked in close harmony with their owners or handlers; strength and independence to dogs that guarded flocks; tenacity and aggressiveness to terriers; and keen eyesight and sense of smell to hounds and sporting dogs.

A breed is a population of dogs that shares a common genetic heritage and passes consistent recognizable traits to the offspring. Thus, a Cocker Spaniel bred to a Cocker Spaniel produces Cocker Spaniel puppies. A Cocker Spaniel bred to a dog of any other breed produces a crossbred dog with some traits from Cocker Spaniels and some from the other parent.

One area of confusion is over the use of the term "hybrid." This, too, is a handy label to use, but it can be misleading. A true hybrid is created by crossing animals of two different species such as a horse and a donkey (mule), a cow and a bison (beefalo), or a lion and a tiger (liger or tigon). Crosses of different animals are generally unable to reproduce but dog breeds and mixes are still dogs, and their offspring have the capacity to reproduce. However, it is now regarded as acceptable to describe crossbred dogs as "hybrids." Another common misperception is over the use of the term "hybrid vigor" to describe crossbreeding of dogs. This implies that crossbred puppies inherit only the best or most desirable traits from each parent. However, it is more than likely that a mix of good and bad traits will surface in the offspring.

Genetics is complicated; research proves that the simple dominance/recessive scheme most of us are familiar with is not applicable in most cases. What you see in the dog is not always what lies below the surface, for the phenotype (appearance) of the dog can hide the genotype (the combination of genes that may or may not be expressed but can be passed on to offspring). The purebred parents of a crossbred dog bring generations of different genetic characteristics to the mix; therefore it is far more difficult to predict

the profile of the cross, understand that all dogs have genetic flaws, and don't fall for uncorroborated claims of perfection for crossbreds. Buyers stand a better chance of getting a healthy puppy that is worth the money if they do so.

There are many misconceptions about crossbred dogs. Chief among them is that the offspring of two different breeds is a breed of its own. Obviously, while it is clever and practical to combine breed names for crossbred puppies, it is inaccurate to say that this new name represents a breed. Only by carefully selecting crossbreds to breed through several generations can breeders produce offspring that qualify as a breed. (See Table C on page 16.)

inherited traits when breeding two crossbred puppies (F2) than it is to forecast the same traits in a purebred puppy.

However, the principle of "hybrid vigor" holds true, i.e., that crossing dogs of known genetic background with dogs of different known genetic background can be used to strengthen beneficial qualities and minimize detrimental ones in offspring. Experienced purebred breeders use this principle when outcrossing (choosing a sire or dam from a different lineage than the breeder's own dogs) to improve certain breed qualities and breed away from others.

The keys to achieving "hybrid vigor" by crossbreeding or outcrossing are "known genetic background" and "experience."

One method that responsible purebred breeders use to gain knowledge about genetic background is to screen parent dogs for inherited diseases. Another is to be aware of health or temperament problems in the previous generations of the dogs they are using. As this book makes clear, the burden is on breeders of crossbreds to do the same, especially if they are using dogs of breeds susceptible to hip dysplasia, luxating patellas, elbow dysplasia, eye diseases, heart abnormalities, or other afflictions for which tests are available.

Designer dogs

The term "designer dogs" is often used as a pejorative term by those who believe that all dog breeding is cruel and abusive and a sign of human vanity. In addition, many of those who promote crossbred dogs market their puppies by giving them amusing "breed" names and alleging that many purebreds have disease and temperament

problems that are fixed by "hybrid vigor" in first-generation crossbreds.

So, given the undertones associated with the term "designer dogs," I was wary about the subject of crossbred dogs. However, this book cuts through the chaff to look at these dogs with a critical eye and a desire to help people make informed choices of a crossbred dog and a crossbred breeder.

The explanation of terms in the beginning of the book sets the stage for anyone who is considering the purchase of a crossbred dog. The chart demonstrating the process of creating a breed from the initial cross is particularly helpful, for it gives potential buyers the inside scoop on the complexity of creating a breed versus the convention of attaching a catchy name to a litter of puppies.

The profiles that form the bulk of the book differentiate between the three types of crossbred dogs—the Australian Labradoodle,

whose breeders are seriously trying to create a new breed; those like the Cockapoo, whose breeders are producing multigenerational puppies but have not yet perfected the cross as a breed; and those like the Goldador, Pekapoo, or Puggle, whose breeders are producing first-generation crosses with no intention to progress to breed status.

Dogs labeled "Labradoodles" could fit into either of the first two categories, depending on the intention of the breeder. Some breeders are crossing Labrador Retrievers and Poodles and labeling the first-generation offspring as Labradoodles, while others have carefully bred generations of dogs that began with the original cross but now, after many generations of careful breeding, produce offspring of predictable appearance, structure, coat, and temperament. Thus, despite their name tag, all Labradoodles are not the same. The phenotype (appearance) of first-generation puppies and dogs may be similar to the phenotype of multi-generational puppies and dogs that meet the definition of a breed, but buyers should ask questions to be sure they are getting what they want, especially if they are interested in breeding their puppy when he is old enough.

The section "Selecting Your Dog" helps prospective buyers determine if they are ready for a crossbred puppy, to choose a reputable breeder, and to select a particular puppy from the litter. It also includes information on choosing a crossbred dog from a shelter and prepares buyers to be interrogated by the breeder or the shelter staff.

The last section is on caring for puppies and adult dogs. An indispensable part of any dog profile book, this section keeps an abundance of valuable information about a chosen dog bound between the same two covers. Thus, the puppy buyer has but to reach for a single volume that covers basic care for his pet and provides suggestions about when to consult a veterinarian for help.

Conclusion

Many breeders of purebreds disdain the efforts of those who crossbreed dogs because they believe that crossbreeding is done for one purpose: to separate unsuspecting buyers from their money. This book helps buyers wend their way through the confusion and sometimes exaggerated claims about crossbreds to select the best crossbred for their families and lifestyles and choose a responsible crossbred breeder. There are obviously many more crossbreds than the ones profiled in the book, but buyers can easily use the same guidelines if they are tempted by any of the others.

Poor choice of a purebred, crossbred, or mixed-breed dog is a major reason for failure of the human/canine bond. People who select the wrong dog for their circumstances are often frustrated that the dog doesn't live up to his potential or his advance billing, and they often respond by sending the dog to a new home, a shelter, or a rescue. Some dogs face the worst fate of all—they die because their owners could not teach them the basic manners needed to blend into the family and the community. In many cases, the fault lies not with the owner or the dog but with the breakdown of the selection process that leads to disappointment and aggravation.

There are more than 300 breeds of dogs in the world. Some folks believe that this number provides more than enough variety, but pet buyers obviously want a wider selection. In addition, many purebreds are rare or are not desirable as pets for certain circumstances or lifestyles. As a result, crossbreds, particularly those that are small-to-medium-sized, fill an important role.

The bottom line for me is that people should have the dog they want, whether that is a purebred, crossbred, or mixed breed, and should take advantage of any and all information that can help them make a wise choice for their circumstances. I hope that those who choose a crossbred dog will do their homework and apply the principles of responsible breeding to the source they select. This book gives them that opportunity.

Explanation of terms

Purebred dogs

Purebred dogs have ancestors that are all of the same standard type produced over many generations. Purebreds were developed for a specific purpose (such as hunting) and for appearance. Typically, dog breeds originated from crossing among populations that were available at the time. Some purebreds were selected from a small gene pool and further selection for standardized characteristics has led to a reduced gene pool in some breeds and the health problems that result from the inbreeding of dogs with genetic defects.

Non-purebred dogs—Crossbreds, mixed breeds, and mongrels

"Crossbred" is the term used for the offspring of two different purebred dogs of different breeds. "Mixed breed" is used for dogs that may be of a recognizable type (Terrier, Spaniel, Retriever, and so on) but with parents of mixed heritage. "Mongrel" is the term used, often in a derogatory way, for dogs of unknown parentage. "Mutt" and "Heinz 57" are some of the nicknames affectionately applied to non-purebred dogs.

Hybrids

Crossbreds are sometimes referred to as "hybrids." Usually a hybrid is the offspring of two different species, but the term can also be used for a cross between two breeds. The term "hybrid" is used in expressions such as "hybrid vigor," in relation to crossbreds.

"Hybrid vigor" (Heterosis)

"Hybrid vigor" is the term used to describe what happens when purebred animals are mated together. When one dog mates with another dog of a different breed, the average performance of their offspring for most traits (such as health and fertility) is greater than the average performance of the two breeds. This superiority in the first generation is called "hybrid vigor" (heterosis).

Designer dog

"Designer dog" refers to the crossbred dogs that have been deliberately developed, particularly in the last decade or two. This light-hearted term is somewhat contentious.

Some dog breeders dislike the pretension and the sense of superiority the label confers on crossbreds, as it implies that only recent crosses have been developed to suit human purposes. On the other hand, serious crossbred breeders also dislike the glibness of the term and the implication that a living creature can be "designed" (and discarded) in the same manner as a handbag.

Recognition of crossbred dogs

Crossbreds are not a "breed." The offspring of two crossbreds will be variable and will not "breed true" like a purebred. Purebred dogs are registered with breed clubs. These clubs produce "breed standards" (the standard by which all dogs in that breed are judged), maintain a studbook, and advance the breed.

Most crossbred dogs do not have their own club or widely recognized standards. One exception is the Australian Labradoodle Association (ALA), an organization with widely recognized standards that has been working on establishing a breed for many years. In the future, selected multigeneration crossbreds such as the Australian Labradoodle may be recognized as a breed by the major kennel clubs, but this will not be the case for most of the crossbreds available today.

Many crossbred dog breeders do not want or plan to develop a breed. Some breeders prefer the apparent health benefits of first-generation dogs. Some prefer to produce varied offspring and are uninterested in the emphasis that breed clubs place on uniformity and show qualities.

Several crossbred clubs are in the early stages of development. Bear in mind that a properly functioning club does more than just "register" your dog for a fee. The club should provide standards, maintain a studbook, and, if promoting multigeneration breeding, have long-term objectives for advancing the crossbred dog.

Dominant and recessive genes

Dogs, like all animals, carry two sets of genes, one from the mother (dam) and one from the father (sire). A dog has some genes that are dominant and other genes that are recessive.

To understand how single genes work we can look at coat color in dogs. The simplified model in Table A shows the possible offspring

KEY
B = black dominant gene   b = brown recessive gene

TABLE A: DOMINANT BLACK COLORATION—POSSIBLE COLORS IN OFFSPRING		
	B parent 2	b parent 2
B parent 1	BB (Black puppy)	Bb (Black puppy)
b parent 1	Bb (Black puppy)	bb (Brown puppy)

This table shows we get three black puppies (BB, Bb and Bb) and one brown puppy (bb). This ratio of 3:1 is known as Mendel's ratio.

The terms used to describe the resulting puppies are as follows:
BB = homozygous black   Bb = heterozygous black   bb = homozygous brown

resulting from the mating of dogs where black coloration is dominant to brown.

If the parent dogs are of different breeds but both breeds carry the same genetic traits, their crossbred offspring will inherit that genetic trait. The trait could be something desirable, like a particular color, or it could be a genetic defect.

Carriers of inherited diseases

All dogs have some genes that are harmful. A defective gene can produce a genetic disease (such as hemophilia). A dog can also be a "carrier," whereby it carries a harmful gene without being affected, yet it can pass on the harmful gene to its offspring and they may be affected, depending on their genetic makeup.

Table B shows how the status of the parents (normal, carrier, or affected) shows up in a proportion of the offspring.

A dominant defective gene will produce disease even if only one copy of the gene is present. These defects are easy to select out of the population and there are few dominant genetic diseases.

A recessive gene will show up in a dog only if both parents carry the gene and the puppy receives two copies of the same gene. These "affected" animals are called "homozygous" for the affected gene.

A puppy carrying one defective recessive gene will appear to be perfectly normal although it will be a "carrier."

A puppy is "normal" for the gene if both its copies of the gene are normal (it is homozygous for the normal gene)—these puppies will never pass on the disease.

Genetic tests for some diseases can identify the three genetic states—normal, carrier, and affected. With this information, the breeder can plan matings that avoid producing affected dogs. If breeders use genetic testing to increase the frequency of normal offspring, this will also help to decrease the frequency of the disease in general.

KEY:
Normal (Clear) = Homozygous for normal gene, so will never develop the disease
Carrier = Carries one disease gene, but will never develop the disease
Affected = Homozygous for the disease gene and will develop the disease

TABLE B: INHERITED RECESSIVE DISEASES

Parent 1	Parent 2		
	Normal	Carrier	Affected
Normal	All = Normal	Half = Normal Half = Carriers	All = Carriers
Carrier	Half = Normal Half = Carriers	Quarter = Normal Half = Carriers Quarter = Affected	Half = Carriers Half = Affected
Affected	All = Carriers	Half = Carriers Half = Affected	All = Affected

Parent breeds, first-generation, and multi-generation dogs

The two different breeds in the initial cross are known as the "parent breeds."

The offspring of the two different dog breeds is a "first-generation" cross. These dogs are labeled (F1). This is short for "first filial generation" —where filial means "brothers" (and sisters).

The first generation is the stage that delivers the greatest benefits of "hybrid vigor." Every (F1) dog has exactly 50 percent of its DNA from each of the parent breeds, making the (F1) dog predictable. There will be some variation in features such as fur type, particularly if the parent breeds have very different fur types.

Most breeders choose to stay breeding first-generation crosses; however, some breeders take on the more complex long-term task of producing "generational" or "multi-generation" dogs.

Second-generation dogs (F2) are the offspring of two first-generation dogs (F1). These (F2) dogs will be far more variable than (F1) dogs, as the variation in the proportion of genes from each parent breed varies. The appearance of (F2) dogs ranges almost across the whole gamut from one parent breed to the other. In the third and subsequent generations the variation is greater than in the (F1) but progressively decreases. By the seventh generation (F7), if the breeding dogs are carefully selected for a particular type, the size and looks of the pups has stabilized with minimal variation.

In theory, by continuing the breeding of unrelated crossbreds of the same combination over successive generations a new breed could be created (see Table C).

TABLE C: CROSSBREEDING THROUGH SEVEN GENERATIONS

(F1)	First generation	Offspring of two different parent breeds, such as: Golden Retriever female x Standard Poodle male producing a Goldendoodle	"Hybrid vigor"—widest gene pool and potential health benefits from crossing two different breeds are most apparent. (F1) puppies tend to be intermediate in characteristics between their parent breeds. (F1) puppies from the same litter will resemble each other, roughly as much as members of an established breed.
(F2)	Second generation	Offspring of two unrelated first-generation crosses, such as: Goldendoodle female x Goldendoodle male producing a Goldendoodle	The appearance of (F2) puppies ranges between one parent breed to the other. (F2) are more likely than (F1) to favor the looks of one of the parent breeds. These are known as "throwbacks" to the parent breed.
(F3)	Third generation	Offspring of two unrelated second-generation crosses, such as: Goldendoodle female x Goldendoodle male producing a Goldendoodle	In the third generation (F3), if a particular type is selected for breeding, fewer "throwback" puppies will occur.
(F4)	Fourth generation	Offspring of two unrelated third-generation crosses, such as: Goldendoodle female x Goldendoodle male producing a Goldendoodle	By the fourth generation (F4) almost no "throwback" puppies will occur. Appearance and personality of puppies becomes more uniform.
(F5)	Fifth generation	Offspring of two unrelated fourth-generation crosses, such as: Goldendoodle female x Goldendoodle male producing a Goldendoodle	By the fifth generation (F5) almost no "throwback" puppies will occur. Appearance and personality of puppies becomes more uniform.
(F6)	Sixth generation	Offspring of two unrelated fifth-generation crosses, such as: Goldendoodle female x Goldendoodle male producing a Goldendoodle	By the sixth generation (F6) almost no "throwback" puppies will occur. Appearance and personality of puppies becomes more uniform.
(F7)	Seventh generation	Offspring of two unrelated sixth-generation crosses, such as: Goldendoodle female x Goldendoodle male producing a Goldendoodle	By the seventh generation (F7) the size and looks of the puppies has stabilized with minimal variation. May be regarded as a breed.

Crossbreeding through generations

The initial (F1) cross shows a relatively high degree of consistency (roughly the same as within an established breed). In theory, if good breeding procedures are maintained over a period of many years there would also be a very high degree of consistency among (F7) dogs. Table C shows a hypothetical example using Goldendoodles. It is in the intervening generations, particularly the second generation, that there is more inconsistency among offspring. For this reason many breeders restrict themselves to crossbreeding (F1) dogs. To get past the less predictable generations such as (F2) and to ensure good breeding lines are maintained requires a large number of dogs to start with and the involvement of many breeders committed to a common goal over years or decades. Inbreeding is very difficult to avoid when developing a new breed unless large numbers of "founder" dogs are used.

The practice of backcrossing (for example, mating a Goldendoodle with an unrelated Poodle to produce a backcrossed Goldendoodle) is sometimes employed by crossbred dog breeders. Backcrossing is used by breeders who are trying to breed puppies with a feature of one parent breed, such as a low-shedding, low-dander coat, or a particular color, or to bring in new bloodlines (see Table D).

TABLE D: BACKCROSSING IN CROSSBREEDING		
(F1)	First generation	Offspring of two different parent breeds, such as: Golden Retriever female x Standard Poodle male producing a Goldendoodle	"Hybrid vigor"—widest gene pool and potential health benefits from crossing two different breeds are most apparent. (F1) puppies tend to be intermediate in characteristics between their parent breeds. (F1) puppies from the same litter will resemble each other, roughly as much as members of an established breed.
(F1B)	First-generation backcross	Offspring of an unrelated first-generation cross and a parent breed dog, such as: Goldendoodle female x Standard Poodle male producing an (F1B) Goldendoodle	(F1B) crosses are more likely to resemble the parent breed involved in the backcross. For example, the likelihood of producing puppies with a low-shedding, low-dander coat is increased by backcrossing to a Standard Poodle but the dog will be lighter framed and longer in the face than an (F1) dog.

Crossbreeding goals

Purebred dogs have been developed over the centuries with a particular function in mind. Crossbred dogs are often criticized for not having a "purpose" in the same manner as purebreds. However, because modern dogs are less likely to be working dogs, their primary function (whether purebred, crossbred, or mongrel) is often as a human companion or family dog. Crossbred breeders aim to produce companion dogs of a particular size with a good temperament, better health, and fewer genetic problems than the parent breed. They may also focus on producing dogs with a specific trait, such as a low-shedding, low-dander coat that is of potential use to allergy sufferers.

Some crossbreds still have a function as working dogs. The Labradoodle was developed decades ago specifically as a guide dog suitable for allergy sufferers. Although inconsistency in that regard meant the breeding program was discontinued,

Labradoodles are still working as guide dogs and more recently Goldendoodles have been trained for guide dog work and other roles. The Goldador is another versatile crossbred and it is used for work as a guide dog, assistance dog, or sniffer dog. Many smaller crossbreds with low-shedding, low-dander coats are used as therapy dogs, as they may be suited to contact with allergy sufferers and the frail aged.

The allergy factor

It cannot be guaranteed that any crossbred dog will not cause allergies in humans. Beware of breeders that claim their dogs are non-allergenic. Even if they claim the dogs are "hypoallergenic" (having relatively low allergenic properties) you will need to make your own decision.

For a start, the offspring of non-shedders may still be shedders. More importantly, shedding is not the only issue to consider as even non-shedding dogs may trigger allergies. Sufferers react to the dust, saliva, dander (dry scales or fluff shed from the skin), and sebum (oily secretions) associated with the hair rather than to the hair itself.

Dander, the top skin layer and certain proteins in saliva, tears, and urine can cause allergic reactions.

The shed hairs attract pollens, dust, mites, and so on, which act as an airborne allergen. Regular washing once a week or fortnight reduces airborne allergens (although dogs shouldn't be washed more than once a week and special moisturizing dog shampoos may be necessary for dogs with sensitive skin).

Always arrange a visit before buying a new puppy or older dog to get an idea of your allergies to the individual dog. However, be

aware that puppy coats change, and allergy-prone people can develop new allergies later in their lives. Allergy-prone people should also follow standard precautions (no dogs in the bedrooms; no dogs on carpets; wash dogs regularly and use coat conditioners to reduce the "dustiness" of the coat; and use an appropriate vaccuum cleaner to prevent distribution of hair and dust mites).

Naming conventions

Some of the popular crossbreds are known by several different names, so this book will list as many of the name variations (with spelling variations) as possible. When conducting Internet searches for information you may need to search each name variation as well as the full name; for example Yorkipoo, Yorkiepoo, and Yorkshire Terrier x Poodle cross.

The Labradoodle

Name variations: *The Australian Labradoodle*

One of the most sought after of all the "designer dogs," the Labradoodle is the captivating result of an initial cross between a Labrador Retriever and a Poodle. A popular and reliable dog, the multi-generation crossbred, the Australian Labradoodle, is being developed as a breed in its own right and may be recognized by kennel clubs in the future.

History of the Labradoodle

In 1989 Wally Conron, breeding manager of the Royal Guide Dogs Associations of Australia in Victoria, produced a litter of puppies by mating a Standard Poodle and a Labrador Retriever. The aim was to produce a dog for vision-impaired people who, because of their allergies to dog hair, had trouble working with regular guide dog breeds.

Sultan, one of the offspring from this first litter, had the desired qualities: an allergy friendly coat, the ability to be trained as a guide dog, and an even temperament. Sultan worked as a companion to a vision-impaired lady in Hawaii for ten years.

Other Australian breeders successfully crossed the initial Labrador and Poodle crossbred. More breeders joined in and, after years of work, it became possible to mate Labradoodles with other Labradoodles. The Labradoodle quickly won people over. The original attraction was to the low-shedding, low-dander coats but increasingly, Labradoodles became popular for their gentle and friendly disposition, trainability, and suitability for working with people. The Royal Guide Dogs Associations no longer breed Labradoodles but some of the Labradoodles they bred many years ago still work for them.

Recognition of breed

A group of Labradoodle breeders known as the Australian Labradoodle Association (ALA) has been working for many years to establish the multi-generation Labradoodle as a recognized breed. ALA recently affiliated with the International Australian Labaradoodle Association (IALA) to bring together breeders

LEFT Multi-generation Australian Labradoodles bred by Cloud Catcher Labradoodles.

FACING PAGE The early-generation Labradoodle was bred from a Labrador and a Poodle by the Royal Guide Dogs Associations of Australia.

Characteristics of the parent breeds

from around the world to unite their breeding programs, to breed for the same goals. IALA is a worldwide body formed to support the future of the Labradoodle and the Australian Labradoodle and to promote awareness. IALA anticipates that in a few years the Australian Labradoodle breed will be recognized by world canine associations.

The Poodle coat is more like wool and sheds little or no hair, offering an ideal balance to the Labrador with its shedding coat. Breeders have focused on producing Labradoodles with a low-shedding, low-dander coat.

First-generation (F1) crossbreeding also provides an opportunity to minimize heritable disorders. Although the Labrador and the Poodle breeds do have some heritable disorders in common, other disorders occur in only one of the parent breeds and so will not be inherited by the first-generation Labradoodle dog.

Labrador Retrievers are intelligent and easily trained. Poodles are also regarded as a highly intelligent dog breed, so the Labradoodle is a smart and easily trained crossbred. The Labradoodle's temperament is also good, as the tendency toward becoming high strung (more common in Toy or Miniature Poodles but it does sometimes occur in Standard Poodles) is tempered by the placid nature of the Labrador. The larger Standard Poodle crosses have an especially good temperament.

Size will vary according to the Poodle parent breed. Standard Poodles produce standard-sized Labradoodles. Miniature

BELOW LEFT: First generation Labradoodle.

BELOW RIGHT: Multi-generation Labradoodle.

FACING PAGE: Multi-generation Labradoodle litter.

Poodles produce medium-sized Labradoodles. Toy Poodles produce Miniature Labradoodles.

First-generation (F1) Labradoodles
Some breeders produce Labradoodles that are first-generation dogs (the direct offspring of a Poodle and a Labrador Retriever). The Labrador is the dam. These dogs are known as Labradoodles.

Multi-generation Labradoodles
Some breeders produce second- or third-generation Labradoodles, or backcrossed dogs. There is less consistency in the (F2) and (F3) generations than in the first cross (F1). The chances of hereditary problems also widen with the (F2) dogs. The significant development with the Labradoodle crossbred is that, over many years, six generations of Labradoodles have been developed in a controlled breeding program. These multi-generation dogs bred and promoted by ALA are known as "Australian Labradoodles."

Apart from just a straightforward cross of the Poodle and the Labrador, with successive

crossings of Labradoodles (see the stages outlined in Table C on page 16) other dog breeds have been bred into the line. These "parent infusion breeds" include: the Irish Water Spaniel, the Curly-Coated Retriever, the American Cocker Spaniel, and the English Cocker Spaniel. The parent infusion breeds were added in order to provide different traits to the initial crossbred. The desired trait from the Irish Water Spaniel is the chocolate-colored coat, from the Curly-Coated Retriever it is the quality low-shedding coat, and from the two types of Cocker Spaniels the desired traits are the boning and continuously growing coat. According to ALA, all the parent breeds and parent infusion breeds bred into the Labradoodle line were carefully selected for exemplary temperament.

Crossbreeding goals

The aim of IALA breeders worldwide is to breed "An all-round great dog that is nonshedding and allergy friendly." Breeders are still working on improving coat types to create a breed that does not shed hair.

Choosing a breeder

The Labradoodle breeding associations, ALA and IALA, can provide contact details for recognized breeders in different countries. Note that there may be long waiting lists for Labradoodle puppies.

Find out if breeders specialize in the first-generation cross, early multi-generation dog, or a later multi-generation dog. If a low-shedding, low-dander dog is a high priority, the later multi-generational Australian Labradoodle, (F4) to (F6), is much more likely to have such a coat.

A reputable breeder will use good breeding stock and select parents on the basis of temperament as well as looks and genetic soundness. The breeder should also provide proof that the puppy's parents were screened for inherited diseases.

Screening tests

Breeders should screen for luxating patellas, hip dysplasia, elbow dysplasia, and eye diseases. (See pages 124 to 125 for more information about screening tests.)

Appearance

Labradoodle characteristics

The Labradoodle has its own distinctive look. The following description is based on the set of guidelines written by ALA. These guidelines are known as a "breed standard." The standard describes the desired appearance of the Australian Labradoodle, a multi-generation dog (F6) developed by breeders over many years. These later multi-generation Australian Labradoodles are more likely to have consistent features than the second- or third-generation dogs.

General appearance

The dog should be athletic and graceful, yet compact, with substance and medium boning.

Size ranges

Standard: height to shoulder between 22 and 26 inches (56 and 66 cm), weight between 55 and 88 pounds (25 and 40 kg).
Medium: height to shoulder between 17 and 22 inches (43 and 56 cm), weight between 44 and 55 pounds (20 and 25 kg).
Miniature: height to shoulder between 13 and 17 inches (33 and 43 cm), weight between 22 and 44 pounds (10 and 20 kg).

Colors

Colors include chalk, cream, gold, apricot, red, black, blue, silver, chocolate, and café. In mature Labradoodles, especially those that enjoy an outdoor lifestyle, the topcoat may show bleaching of color and discoloration, referred to as "sunning."

Body

Height to length ratio should be 10 to 12
(being slightly longer in leg than body) but
still appearing compact. Shoulders should
have good angulation with firm elbows.
Upright shoulders are a fault. Hindquarters
should be of medium angulation with short,
strong hocks.

Coat

Coat length should be 4 to 6 inches
(10 to 15 cm) long. It should be straight,
wavy, or forming light loose spirals. It
should not be too thick or dense nor
should it be fluffy or fuzzy. It should be
a single coat. Any sign of a double coat
is a fault. Coats consist of hair, fleece, or
wool (see page 29 for details). Hair is a
temporary coat and should be bred
away from.

Tail

Preferred low set and saber-like,
a high-set tail is permissible.
Possum type or teapot handle
tails are a fault. Padded, heavy
or coarse appearance is a fault.

Legs

Movement when trotting should be strong, with good reach and drive,
giving the appearance of "going somewhere." When relaxed or at play
they will prance and skim the ground lightly. Top line should remain
level with strong loin and croup. They are a galloping dog; therefore
flanks should rise up from a deep brisket and well-sprung ribs.

Living with your Labradoodle

The behavior and temperament of Labradoodles make them ideal pets for owners prepared for the responsibilities of grooming and training. They are long-living and have a great desire to be part of the family. As Labradoodles are highly intelligent dogs, good management in the early years is essential.

General behavior

According to ALA's *Breed Standard of the Australian Labradoodle*, the Labradoodle should be joyful and energetic when free, and soft and quiet when handled. It should approach people in a happy, friendly manner with eye-to-eye contact, be eager and easy to train.

Activity levels

A daily walk is recommended. At times, Labradoodles may be overly active, but this behavior is more common in the early-generation dogs.

Barking

Labradoodles are not known to be barking dogs but individual dogs will vary. They may bark when ignored or ostracized from the family.

Temperament

Labradoodles are affectionate and amiable in character. They enjoy being with people, making them ideal companions. The temperament of a dog is directly related to parentage, so discrepancies can exist with any crossbred dog.

Other pets

Labradoodles should not show aggression toward other dogs. When properly trained they are good with other pets.

Children

Labradoodles are known to be gentle with children but, as with all dogs, supervision and training are recommended.

Trainability

Labradoodles are intelligent dogs that have a high aptitude for training. They benefit greatly from obedience training as they are best not left to get bored.

Working

The intelligence and tenacity of the Labradoodle, combined with its love of people, makes it suitable for work as a therapy dog. Labradoodles

VET'S ADVICE

Allergies

Labradoodles and many other crossbred dogs are popular because it is believed that they are less likely to cause allergies in people. See the section on page 18 for an explanation of how allergies work and the factors to consider.

were originally developed for guide dog work; some vision-impaired guide dog users have Labradoodles that have worked with them for more than ten years.

General health and lifespan

Labradoodles are generally healthy dogs that live for around 12 to 14 years.

Skin problems are the most commonly reported condition. Labradoodles can also have a problem with ear infections, so regular cleaning and plucking of the ear canal is recommended.

Eye problems are relatively common, especially if hair/excessive eyelashes get near the eyes. Both the Labrador Retriever and Poodle parent breeds can have the genetic disorder prcd-PRA, so it may be a problem in the Labradoodle. This disorder causes progressive rod-cone degeneration in the eye leading to declining vision and eventual blindness. Genetic testing can assist in making a diagnosis of prcd-PRA.

Other health problems that may be experienced by the Labradoodle could include epilepsy, diabetes, patellar

luxation (a knee problem), hip dysplasia, elbow dysplasia, allergies, and hypothyroidism.

Space needs

A Labradoodle living in a reasonably sized backyard or garden should still be walked every day. Crate training may be helpful as Labradoodles are happy to sleep in small, sheltered spaces. However, it is important that they are correctly introduced to the crate or the carrier.

Grooming

Many Labradoodles have a single coat. Coats vary from short and coarse to long and curly, so grooming requirements vary. Dogs that don't shed require regular clipping and brushing.

Coat types

Hair has the texture of typical dog hair. It is a shedding coat and has several different looks ranging from sparse feathering on the legs and a bearded face to a shaggy all-over look. It can shed in varying degrees but no matter the quantity of hair, any coat that sheds is considered a hair coat. Breeders of the multi-generation Australian Labradoodle are breeding away from the hair coat.

Fleece is a very soft coat that has close to the same texture as an angora goat. It is a nonshedding coat and can either have a straight or wavy look or a soft, spiraling curl look. This coat is an easy-to-manage coat and is highly prized by Labradoodle breeders.

Wool is reminiscent of a sheep's wool in texture. This is a nonshedding coat and can have a highly prized looser spiraling look that opens up easily to the skin, a tight dense curling look, or a thick and very dense straighter look. It is recommended to breed away from the thick and dense wool coat, as such coats are very high maintenance compared to the looser spiraling wool.

The Goldador

Name variations: *Golden Labrador, Glab, Retrievador*

The Goldador is a cross between a Golden Retriever and a Labrador Retriever—two similar and extremely popular dog breeds. These large dogs are both known for their intelligence, responsiveness, and obedience. Ideally, the Goldador combines the high tolerance level of the Labrador with the sensitivity of the Golden Retriever. As well as being a devoted family pet, the Goldador is highly regarded as a working dog, especially as a guide dog.

History of the Goldador

Goldadors are less well known than the many Poodle crossbreds, but for more than a decade Goldadors have been deliberately bred by organizations to work as guide dogs, search and rescue dogs, support dogs, and drug detection dogs. Goldadors have also become popular as family pets.

Recognition of breed

There is no official breed standard for the Goldador. Guide dog organizations usually prefer to use first-generation crossbreds.

Characteristics of the parent breeds

Labradors tend to be good with children and not easily alarmed. However, they can be very independent. Golden Retrievers tend to be loving dogs, but they can be socially demanding and find it difficult to be left alone. The coat of the Golden Retriever can be difficult to look after. A Goldador with good parentage that combines the best traits of both parent breeds should have sociability, independence, and trainability—and an easily groomed coat.

The Goldador may also inherit health problems, such as PRA (Progressive Retinal Atrophy) and hip joint arthritis, that both parents have in common.

First-generation (F1) Goldadors

Goldadors are usually first-generation crossbreds. Guide dog associations have bred excellent working guide dogs from the first crosses of purebred Labrador Retriever with purebred Golden Retriever. Either breed can be the sire or the dam.

ABOVE First-generation Goldador puppy from a Golden Retriever sire and Labrador Retriever dam.

Multi-generation Goldadors

Multi-generation Goldadors are not common. Guide dog trainers prefer to work with first-generation crosses because second-generation dogs may display temperament problems. First-generation guide dogs are usually neutered and so will not breed further.

Crossbreeding goals

As a family pet, the Goldador probably resulted from the natural mixing of two similar dogs that are much loved by the general public. Labrador Retrievers recently topped the American Kennel Club's most popular dog list and the Golden Retriever came second (Source: *American Kennel Club's 2004 Registration Statistics*).

The Goldador's attributes make it an effective working dog. In the study *Crossbreeding to Improve Temperament - August 1993*, the Guide Dogs Association (UK) rated the Golden Retriever x Labrador Retriever cross as its most successful dog, ahead of the parent breeds and ahead of other purebreds, such as the German Shepherd Dog, or Border Collie (see <www.gdba.org.uk> for details).

The breeding of guide dogs is a far more exacting process than breeding family pets. The working Goldador must be bred from good lines and trained thoroughly then matched to the requirements of the handler. Because the upper age range of people who have been given guide dogs is increasing, guide dog organizations may be especially interested in easily managed Goldadors.

Choosing a breeder

There is no Goldador Club. Guide dog associations may be worth contacting for advice on reputable Goldador breeders.

ABOVE Adult first-generation Goldador bred and trained in guiding by Guide Dogs Queensland.

A reputable breeder will use good breeding stock and select parents on the basis of temperament as well as looks and genetic soundness. The breeder should also provide proof that the puppy's parents were screened for inherited diseases.

Screening tests

Breeders should screen for eyes disorders (including juvenile cataracts), PRA, and hip and elbow dysplasia. (See pages 124 to 125 for more information about screening tests.)

Other popular Labrador crosses	
Labrador Retriever x Beagle	Labbe
Labrador Retriever x Border Collie	Border Retriever
Labrador Retriever x Cocker Spaniel	Spanador

31

Appearance

Goldador characteristics
There is no official breed standard for the Goldador. The following are characteristics of a typical first-generation dog.

General appearance
The first-generation cross will produce a dog that resembles the Golden Retriever as a very young puppy but looks very much like a Labrador as it matures.

Tail
The tail sometimes has more feathering than that of a purebred Labrador.

Size ranges
As a cross of two larger breeds, the Goldador is on average about 22 to 24 inches (56 to 61 cm) height to shoulder and weighs about 60 to 80 pounds (27 to 36 kg).

Colors
Goldadors are mostly yellow but can be any shade of gold, or red to yellow, and black.

Ears
Ears vary but are generally slightly longer than the Labrador's ears.

Nose
The Goldador's nose is narrower than that of the Labrador.

Coat
The Goldador has the Labrador's smooth, short-haired double coat, without the heavy feathering of many Golden Retrievers.

Build
As Goldadors mature they resemble Labradors, especially as they bulk out around the shoulders.

Living with your Goldador

Goldadors are loving and highly devoted to their owners so they make attentive family pets. As working dogs, Goldadors are described as confident and easy to train.

General behavior

Goldador owners and trainers report that Goldadors are good dogs that are sociable but also show independence.

Activity levels

Goldadors need daily exercise to avoid weight gain. They enjoy retrieving balls and other toys, and swimming.

Barking

Goldadors are not known to be big barkers.

Temperament

As a family pet, Goldadors tend to be loving, highly devoted to their owners, and willing to please. Goldadors can be

reserved with strangers and are sometimes one-person dogs.

To work as guide dogs Goldadors need to enjoy human company, be calm in public, and love retrieving. Traits such as anxiousness are not desirable. Goldadors have been used successfully in working situations where confidence and initiative are required.

The temperament of a dog is directly related to parentage, so discrepancies can exist with any crossbred dog.

Other pets

Goldadors are generally good with other pets.

Children

Goldadors are generally good with children but, as with all dogs, supervision and training are recommended.

VET'S ADVICE

Obesity and heatstroke

Goldadors are very inquisitive and love to eat things they shouldn't! Take care to prevent young Goldadors from consuming foreign bodies (such as toys or socks) and possible toxins (such as chocolate or snail bait). As they get older, they can often get pancreatitis if they get too much fat in their diet, so what you feed your Goldador is very important.

Any dog of any age can get heatstroke but take special care with the Goldador, especially the older or overweight dog. Dogs should never be left in a car and never overexercised on hot days. Water should always be available and a cool hose will reduce the dog's temperature on hot days. Heatstroke can be fatal and can be first seen by excessive panting, salivation, and anxiety. Immediate veterinary treatment is required. Do not put your dog in freezing cold water in these circumstances. Call the veterinarian first for advice if you are a long way from the nearest veterinary hospital.

Trainability

Goldadors are easily trained.

Working

Different organizations value Goldadors for their work as guide dogs, sniffer dogs, search and rescue dogs, and therapy dogs. A well-trained Goldador is an asset when dealing with vision-impaired people who are frail or have special needs or disabilities. Goldadors currently work for organizations such as the Guide Dogs Association (UK), Guide Dogs Queensland (Australia), and Southeastern Guide Dogs (United States). Australian Support Dogs, NSW and Queensland, have used the Goldador as an assistance dog for the past five years.

General health and lifespan

The average lifespan of a Goldador is approximately

10 to 14 years. Health problems may include ear and skin infections, PRA, and other eye disorders. The parent breeds, and therefore the Goldador, may carry centralized PRA or Retinal Pigment Epithelial Dystrophy (RPED), with changes in the center of the retina leading to gradual loss of vision.

Hip and elbow dysplasia may affect the Goldador. Both Labradors and Golden Retrievers have a high incidence of hip dysplasia, the main cause of hip joint arthritis later in life. The hips of the Goldador will reflect the hips of both its parents and its own upbringing (environmental factors).

Goldadors can be prone to obesity from a young age if they are overfed and not well exercised, as they may have a lower metabolic rate than other dogs. Being overweight puts the heart and joints under great stress as the dog ages and may be associated with diabetes.

Space needs

Goldadors thrive most with an average-sized backyard or garden. Apartment-dwelling dogs require lots of exercise.

Grooming

Goldadors are prone to shedding. However, the smooth, short-haired double coat of the Goldador is easy to groom and requires little maintenance. Comb and brush with a firm, bristle brush and pay attention to the undercoat. Bathe or dry shampoo only when necessary. The ears should be checked and cleaned properly to avoid problems.

The Cockapoo

Name variations: *Spoodle, Cock-A-poo, Cockerpoo*

The engaging result of a cross between a Cocker Spaniel and a Poodle, the Cockapoo has actually been a popular dog for decades. There are two types of Cockapoo. The American Cockapoo is an American Cocker Spaniel crossed with a Poodle. The second is the English Cockapoo, an English Cocker Spaniel crossed with a Poodle—in many countries it is also known as the Spoodle.

History of the Cockapoo

The Cockapoo is one of the older designer dogs. Rather than being a new fad, the Cockapoo has been bred since at least the 1950s. Because it has no undercoat, the Cockapoo sheds less than a Cocker Spaniel, making the crossbred a potentially good option for allergy sufferers and a popular companion pet and family dog.

The original matings were probably accidental but the intelligence and low-shedding, low-dander coat of the Poodle combined with the especially laid-back, devoted nature of the Spaniel has won over the public. Cockapoos now come in a variety of sizes and in any color that comes from the Cocker Spaniel or the Poodle.

Recognition of breed

There is no official breed standard for the Cockapoo. To avoid the irresponsible and unplanned breeding that has occurred in the past, the Cockapoo Club of America (CCA) has been founded. The aim of the CCA is to help the CCA American Cockapoo and the CCA English Cockapoo become a recognized breed by "selectively breeding unrelated pairs bred for health and temperament down the generations."

The CCA differentiates between the American and the English Cockapoo because the American and the English Cocker Spaniel are two separate breeds. The CCA recommends that the crossbreds should not be bred with each other, that is, a CCA American Cockapoo must only be bred with an unrelated, qualifying CCA American Cockapoo, not crossed with a CCA English Cockapoo.

LEFT Young cream and black coated first-generation Cockapoos.

FACING PAGE Adult first-generation Cockapoo with cream coat.

The Cockapoo Club of America has strict breeding standards for their breeder members (see the Web site <www.cockapooclub.com> for more details). The CCA recommends breeding together only unrelated American Cockapoos or unrelated English Cockapoos that have been selectively chosen for health and temperament and have passed annual CERF exams and OFA patellar luxation exams (at a minimum), and meet the breed standard for the American or English Cockapoo.

Characteristics of the parent breeds

The Cockapoo derives its high intelligence from the Poodle. Another asset from the Poodle is the low-shedding, low-dander coat. This makes the Cockapoo a potentially good option for people who have problems with allergies.

The sweet and patient disposition often associated with the Cocker Spaniel is apparent in the Cockapoo offspring, provided that both of the parent breeds have been selected on the basis of temperament.

English Cockers are often used as the Cocker parent breed because they have fewer health and temperament problems than the American Cocker, but American Cockers are popular parent breeds in the United States.

First-generation (F1) Cockapoos
Many Cockapoos are first generation (the direct offspring of a Poodle and Cocker Spaniel). For breeding English Cockapoos either parent breed can be the sire or dam but the English Cocker Spaniel is usually used as the dam due to size differences.

For breeding American Cockapoos either parent breed can be the dam but the American Cocker Spaniel is usually the dam due to size differences. However, the standard-sized American Cockapoo is bred from a Standard Poodle dam and an American Cocker Spaniel sire. This size is popular for people with allergies who want a large dog (weighing up to 46 pounds or 21 kg).

Multi-generation Cockapoos
The CCA supports the breeding of multi-generation Cockapoos and encourages breeders to keep detailed breeding records. Statistically, in the CCA breeding program for a second-generation (F2) breeding, one in eight have the Cocker look; one in eight the Poodle look; and six in eight the standard Cockapoo or "Benji" look. Subsequent generations show an increasing proportion of Cockapoos with the standard look.

Crossbreeding goals
The Cockapoo has been developed as a low-shedding, low-dander, mellow family dog with good health. The CCA recommends selective breeding down the generations of non-related pairs with the goal of enhancing "the desired characteristics of the Cockapoo in the succeeding generations."

Choosing a breeder
The CCA can provide the contact details for recognized Cockapoo breeders in the United

ABOVE LEFT Cream adult English Cockapoo (Spoodle).

BELOW LEFT Adult Cockapoo featuring black and tan coat.

ABOVE Cream first-generation English Cockapoo (Spoodle) puppy.

States. In addition, the CCA office can verify a CCA Star Rated Breeder's documentation (Email <office@cockapooclub.com>).

In other countries, breeders of other poodle crossbreds may help locate reputable breeders of Cockapoos.

A reputable breeder will use good breeding stock and select parents on the basis of temperament as well as looks and genetic soundness. The breeder should also provide proof that the puppy's parents were screened for inherited diseases.

Screening tests

Breeders should screen for eye diseases, and for potential hip and elbow problems, as well as luxating patellas.

Both the Cocker and the Poodle are prone to inherited eye diseases. Cockapoo breeders should have regular ophthalmological examinations of their breeding stock to certify that the dogs are free of eye diseases. This creates a better chance of getting a crossbred puppy that will not develop possibly painful and extensive eye disease later on. The CCA recommends that all breeding dogs should be certified annually by the Canine Eye Registration Foundation as being free of genetic eye disease.

Other OFA certifications and databases include congenital cardiac, thyroid, hip, and elbow. Breeders who are breeding larger Cockapoos from Standard Poodles are encouraged to do OFA hip certification. (See pages 124 to 125 for more information about screening tests.)

Appearance

Cockapoo characteristics

The CCA encourages all Cockapoo breeders to hold health and temperament first and foremost and to aim for a dog with a "calm and mellow disposition; sweet and patient nature; intelligence; loyalty; friendliness; sturdiness, stamina, and good health." The following is based on the guidelines or "Breed Standards" written by the CCA.

General appearance

A dog that does not resemble either of the originating breeds. Unclipped/scissored in full coat, it has the general "Benji" appearance.

Size ranges

Standard: height to shoulder more than 19 inches (48 cm), weight 30 pounds or more (13.6 kg).
Mini standard: height to shoulder between 15 and 19 inches (38 and 48 cm), weight between 20 and 30 pounds (9 and 13.6 kg).
Miniature: height to shoulder between 10 and 15 inches (26 and 38 cm), weight between 10 and 20 pounds (4.5 and 9 kg).

Colors

All colors and combinations are acceptable. White is an accompanying color rather than a base color.

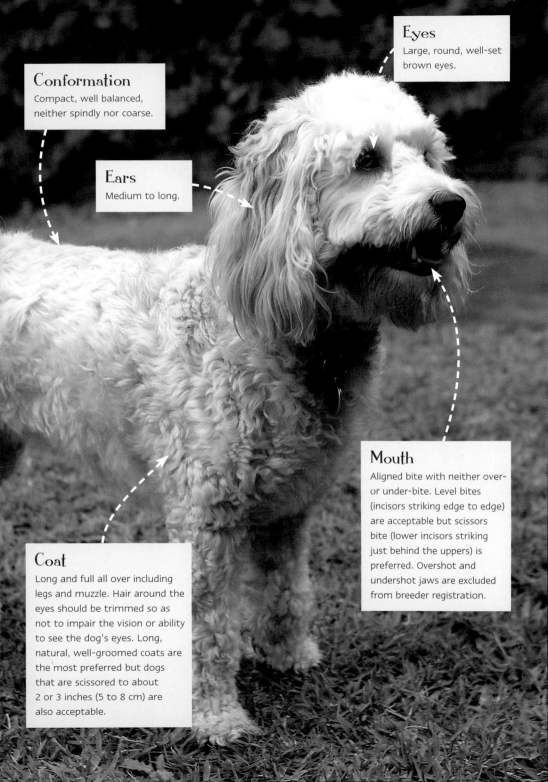

Eyes
Large, round, well-set brown eyes.

Conformation
Compact, well balanced, neither spindly nor coarse.

Ears
Medium to long.

Mouth
Aligned bite with neither over- or under-bite. Level bites (incisors striking edge to edge) are acceptable but scissors bite (lower incisors striking just behind the uppers) is preferred. Overshot and undershot jaws are excluded from breeder registration.

Coat
Long and full all over including legs and muzzle. Hair around the eyes should be trimmed so as not to impair the vision or ability to see the dog's eyes. Long, natural, well-groomed coats are the most preferred but dogs that are scissored to about 2 or 3 inches (5 to 8 cm) are also acceptable.

Living with your Cockapoo

Cockapoos are said to be "...eager to please, easily trained, vigorous, clean, healthy, and long lived" (CCA). The dog's flexibility and range of sizes make it ideal for a number of special situations. Its ability to relate to people and children make it highly prized as a family dog.

General behavior

Cockapoo owners report that their dogs are friendly, spirited, outgoing, and loving. They love humans and attention so are best included in family activities rather than left in the backyard or garden.

Activity levels

Cockapoos are mellow but playful dogs that will enjoy fetching, running, walking, and trips to the park.

Barking

Barking varies with different dogs but Cockapoos may bark if left alone as they are bred to be companions.

Temperament

Cockapoos are said to be bright, friendly dogs that get on well with people. American Cocker dams and studs should be screened and chosen for health and temperament. The American Cockapoo is reported to be calmer than the American Cocker parent breed. "Cocker rage" syndrome or unpredictable, at times aggressive, temperament may occur if the parent dog is from poorly bred stock.

English Cocker x Poodle crosses (Spoodles) may have fewer health and temperament problems than American Cocker x Poodle crosses. Discrepancies can occur with any dog. Selecting the parent dogs specifically for health and temperament is the most important factor, as the temperament of any dog is directly related to parentage.

Cockapoos are generally good with other pets. They are friendly when socialized with other animals, such as cats, especially when they grow up with them from puppyhood.

Children

Given their parent breeds, Cockapoos get on well with children; but, as with all dogs, supervision and training are recommended.

Trainability

Training is important. The time and energy owners put into their Cockapoo puppies will be rewarded by well-trained, well-loved family members.

Working

Cockapoos are sometimes used as therapy dogs. Their low-shedding, low-dander coats provide an advantage when working with people as they don't tend to cause allergic reactions in the patients they visit. They are not suited to work as hunting or herding dogs.

General health and lifespan

The average lifespan of a Cockapoo is about 12 to 15 years. Health problems to watch for include cataracts, juvenile cataracts, any eye disease carried by the Cocker or the Poodle, patellar luxation, liver disease, ear infections, and skin allergies.

Different eye diseases show up at different ages in different breeds. As two different breeds are involved, diligent checking for genetic diseases is required to avoid them at all costs. Both breeders and the public should request CERF exams on the parent dogs before they purchase a puppy to prove the dogs are healthy.

Hip dysplasia is not a common problem in the mini and smaller Cockapoos. However, before using a Standard Poodle to breed Cockapoos, the hips of the Poodle should first be certified.

In general, Standard Poodles actually have fewer genetic problems than the smaller breeds of Poodles and Cockers so their crosses are less likely to have problems.

Space needs

Cockapoos vary in sizes but medium-sized dogs will adapt to an average backyard or garden. Miniature and smaller Cockapoos adapt well to small living spaces such as apartments.

Grooming

The desired coat of the first-generation Cockapoo is wavy, with loose, fluffy curls but not curled as tightly as the Poodle coat and not straight like some Cocker Spaniel coats. Grooming may take between 5 and 15 minutes per day. Thick and wavy coats may require a "slicker" brush to take out loose or matted hair. Professional grooming every four to six weeks is recommended. Dogs with a more Poodle-like coat (such as some second-generation Cockapoos) may need clipping.

Watch the eyes for weeping. Eye tearing can be gently wiped away with a warm, damp washcloth daily, if necessary. Hair should be scissored back so as not to obstruct the dog's eyes or vision.

Ear infections

The Cockapoo, as with many dogs with pendulous ears, may have decreased aeration of the ear canal and is sometimes prone to seborrhea, bacterial, or fungal infections that can lead to otitis (ear inflammation/infection). In cases of chronic otitis, surgery may be required to help improve the clinical signs. The owner can use a veterinarian-recommended ear cleaning solution with an ear drying agent in it as often as once or twice a week to keep ear problems at bay. Professional grooming can eliminate or greatly reduce ear infections from Cockapoos whose owners fail to keep the ear canal free of hair, clean, and dry. The fur under the ear flap can be shaved closer to help aerate the ear.

The Schnoodle

An attractive dog with a low-shedding coat, the Schnoodle is a cross between a Poodle and a Schnauzer. As there are three different Schnauzer breeds and three different Poodle breeds, size and temperament depend on the type of Poodle and the type of Schnauzer used to produce the Schnoodle.

History of the Schnoodle
The Schnoodle has attracted attention since at least the 1980s when consumer demand for Poodle crosses began to increase. The Schnoodle's appeal is enhanced by a low-shedding, low-dander coat, intelligence and trainability. Smaller Schnoodles resulting from smaller parent breeds are ideal lapdogs.

Recognition of breed
There is no official breed standard for the Schnoodle.

Characteristics of the parent breeds
The Schnoodle benefits from the intelligence of both the Poodle and the Schnauzer parent breeds. Another advantage is that the low-shedding, low-dander coat of the Poodle and the single, low-shedding coat of the Schnauzer results in a low-shedding coat, making the Schnoodle a potentially good option for people who have problems with allergies.

Parents may be a Toy Poodle, Miniature Poodle, or Standard Poodle crossed with a Miniature Schnauzer, Standard Schnauzer, or Giant Schnauzer. Ideally, the Schnauzer parent should be mated with a dog of a corresponding size; for example, a Miniature Schnauzer with a Toy Poodle producing a Miniature Schnoodle of less than 12 inches (31 cm) in height to shoulder.

The Schnauzer x Poodle cross is more likely to have a reliable temperament than the Schnauzer parent breed, which tends to be tough, rowdy, and protective of territory.

First-generation (F1) Schnoodles
Most Schnoodles are first generation (the direct offspring of a Poodle and Schnauzer). Either breed can be the sire or dam, depending on relative sizes.

Multi-generation Schnoodles
Breeders in the United States have begun to develop carefully documented multi-generational Schnoodles with a view to establishing multi-generational lines.

Crossbreeding goals

The Schnoodle was developed to be a low-shedding, midsized, long-lived family dog with minimal health problems. Some Schnoodle breeders in the United States are working on proposed guidelines for future development of the Schnoodle as a breed.

Choosing a breeder

Breeders of other Poodle crossbreds may help locate reputable breeders of Schnoodles.

ABOVE Gray first-generation adult Schnoodle.

OPPOSITE Black first-generation Schnoodle puppy.

A reputable breeder will use good breeding stock and select parents on the basis of temperament as well as looks and genetic soundness. The breeder should also provide proof that the puppy's parents were screened for inherited diseases.

Screening tests

Breeders of Schnoodles should screen the breeding dogs for eye diseases and potential hip and elbow problems. Breeders should also screen for luxating patellas. (See pages 124 to 125 for more information about screening tests.)

Appearance

Schnoodle characteristics

There is no official breed standard for the Schnoodle. The following characteristics can be seen in a typical first-generation (F1) Schnoodle.

General appearance

The Schnoodle inherits the general looks and apppearance of the Schnauzer.

Tail
The Schnoodle has an overcurled tail.

Build
The Schnoodle has the finer bones of the Poodle.

Size ranges

Because of the different Schnauzer and Poodle sizes there is a range of Schnoodle sizes. Early-generation breedings may also make it difficult to predict sizes. For a mini-Schnoodle with a height to shoulder under 12 inches (31cm), a general guide to weight would be 10 pounds (4.5 kg) and under. For a Standard Schnoodle with a height to shoulder of 15 inches (38 cm) or more, the weight would be 13 to 20 pounds (5.9 to 9 kg).

Colors

Schnoodles come in gray, silver, and black, sometimes with a white harlequin mask. Occasionally the Schnoodle develops the Schnauzer silvering as it matures.

Ears
The ears are in the same position as the Schnauzer.

Eyes
The eyes are bifocal and close to each other.

Nose
The nose has a square look, like the Schnauzer nose.

Mouth
The mouth is more like the Schnauzer, with a square jaw.

Coat
The coat is soft and wavy, similar to that of a baby Schnauzer rather than ringleted or tightly curled like the Poodle, or as coarse as the Schnauzer coat.

Legs
The Schnoodle has the finer legs of the Poodle.

Living with your Schnoodle

Schnoodles are said to be easy to train, generally happy and affectionate, energetic, intelligent, obedient, playful, and alert. As most Schnoodles like to be around people, they can be good family pets and companions as well as security dogs.

General behavior
Schnoodle owners report that their dogs are loving, loyal, happy, active, and protective.

Activity levels
Activity levels will depend on parentage and size, but in general, Schnoodles appreciate brisk daily walks and off-leash games. Many Schnoodles also love the water.

Barking
Some Schnoodles will become yappy if not trained correctly or if left outside alone while the family is indoors.

Temperament
Schnoodles are generally clever and affectionate dogs with a happy temperament. Schnoodles are often very protective of family members, but this can become problematic if the dog becomes too attached.

Larger varieties of Schnoodles (including crosses of the Giant Schnauzer and the Standard Poodle) have the best temperament and should produce a quieter, more relaxed, intelligent dog.

The temperament of a dog is directly related to parentage, so discrepancies can exist with any crossbred dog.

Other pets
Schnoodles often prefer to live with people than with other dogs. They are best not left unattended with cats and other small animals.

Children
Schnoodles are often more comfortable with adults than with children. As with all dogs, supervision and training are

VET'S ADVICE

Digging
Schnoodles can acquire the bad behavior of digging but additional training, attention, and exercise can often stop this.

recommended and Schnoodles will require training from an adult person. Over time they can become good family dogs, but Schnoodles will also thrive in single or couple adult households.

Trainability

Schnoodles are generally intelligent, responsive, and easy to train. They are movement-motivated rather than treat-motivated and have a great potential for agility and learning new tricks. As the Schnauzer parent breed can be quite dominant, early obedience training is advisable, especially for the larger Schnoodles.

Working

Schnoodles are sometimes used as therapy dogs. Their low-shedding, low-dander coats provide an advantage when working with people. The working potential of this relatively new crossbred is unknown, but breeders report that Schnoodles are protective of their family, so make good security dogs, and also have good hunting skills.

General health and lifespan

The average lifespan for a Schnoodle is approximately 10 to 15 years but parentage is one factor that will influence longevity. Larger varieties (crosses of the Giant Schnauzer and the Standard Poodle) are more robust.

Health problems include eye problems, patellar luxation (a knee problem), hip dysplasia, and Legg-Calvé-Perthes disease (a genetic hip-joint disease). Schnoodles may be susceptible to skin conditions experienced by the Schnauzer parent breed. Like the Poodle parent breed, Schnoodles, as they age, are more prone to cataracts, heart disease, diabetes, other endocrine diseases, skin problems, and dental disease. Both parent breeds have a reasonable incidence of epilepsy and congenital eye defects so these could afflict the Schnoodle.

Space needs

Space needs vary according to the dog's size, but medium-sized dogs will adapt to an average backyard or garden.

Grooming

A first-generation (F1) Schnoodle will have a soft wavy coat that is relatively high maintenance and requires weekly brushing. These Schnoodles have low dander and shed little hair, so are potentially good for allergy sufferers, but weekly bathing is sometimes recommended.

Second-generation (F2) Schnoodle coats will vary from the Poodle's curls to the hard, straight hair of the Schnauzer or anything in between. Schnoodles that inherit the Poodle's coat need to have their coats clipped every 6 to 12 weeks.

The Goldendoodle

Name variations: *Groodle*

A relatively recent addition to the Poodle crossbreds, Goldendoodles are the beautiful result of crossing a Poodle with a Golden Retriever. Similar to the Labradoodle, the Goldendoodle also offers the benefits of high intelligence and a potentially low-shedding, low-dander coat.

low-dander coat have drawn dog lovers to the Goldendoodle, particularly in Australia and North America. Goldendoodles are now bred in different size ranges, including Standard and Miniature.

Recognition of breed

There is no official breed standard for the Goldendoodle. Most breeders provide first-generation crosses.

History of the Goldendoodle

The Goldendoodle crossbred originated in North America. During the 1990s Goldendoodles emerged as an alternative to the Labradoodle and the Cockapoo, though initially offering a larger dog than the Cockapoo. The appeal of a friendly, intelligent dog and the prospect of a low-shedding,

Characteristics of the parent breeds

The first generation Goldendoodle usually inherits the woolly, low-shedding, low-dander coat of the Poodle rather than the double coat of the Golden Retriever. This makes the Goldendoodle a potentially good option for allergy sufferers.

As the product of two clever parent breeds, the Goldendoodle crossbred is also highly intelligent and easy to train. The Poodle and the Golden Retriever have been in the top five list of trainable dogs (*The Intelligence of Dogs: Canine Consciousness and Capabilities*, Stanley Coren, The Free Press, 1994).

Sizes vary according to the Poodle parent breed. Standard Poodles produce large Standard Goldendoodles. Miniature Poodles produce medium Standard Goldendoodles and Toy Poodles produce Miniature Goldendoodles.

LEFT First-generation Goldendoodle puppy with golden coat.

FACING PAGE First-generation Miniature Goldendoodle with golden coat.

Working dogs

Goldendoodles have been successfully trained as working dogs.

ABOVE Jamie, a three-quarter Golden Retriever Goldendoodle (bred and donated by DoodleQuest) is being trained by certified pet dog trainer Carole Schatz. Jamie works as a therapy dog as well as a service and working dog. He is part of a peanut allergy research study learning to sniff and detect peanut allergens in human food.

ABOVE Richter the Goldendoodle (bred and donated by Fox Creek Farm) was trained at Guide Dogs of America in Sylmar, California (in the city of Los Angeles). Richter has worked as a guide dog since 2005.

RIGHT Murphy Brown (bred by Kate's Family Pets) was trained by Velma's Pets as Therapy to work as a therapy dog.

First-generation (F1) Goldendoodles

Goldendoodles are first-generation crosses (the direct offspring of a Poodle and a Golden Retriever). The Golden Retriever is the dam.

Multi-generation Goldendoodles

Some breeders have developed second generation (F2) Standard and Miniature Goldendoodles but (unlike the Labradoodle) the Goldendoodle has not yet been developed as a multi-generation crossbred. Backcrossing is sometimes used to produce (F1B) Goldendoodles with a more poodle-like coat.

Crossbreeding goals

The Goldendoodle was developed for its low-shedding, low-dander coat, trainability, and aptitude for family life.

Choosing a breeder

Breeders of other Poodle crossbreds may be able to help with locating reputable breeders of Goldendoodles.

A reputable breeder will use good breeding stock and select parents on the basis of temperament as well as looks and genetic soundness. The breeder should also provide proof that the puppy's parents were screened for inherited diseases.

Screening tests

Breeders of Goldendoodles should screen their breeding stock for heart problems, luxating patellas, hip dysplasia, elbow dysplasia, and eye diseases. (See pages 124 to 125 for more information about screening tests.)

ABOVE First generation Standard Goldendoodle with mainly white coat.

❀ Appearance

Goldendoodle characteristics

There is no official breed standard for the Goldendoodle. The following are characteristics of a typical first-generation (F1) Goldendoodle.

General appearance

The Goldendoodle resembles both the Poodle and the Golden Retriever.

Build

The build of the Goldendoodle resembles that of the Golden Retriever.

Tail

The tail may be level but will sometimes curl over the back.

Size ranges

Goldendoodles now come in several sizes, for example:
Large standard: height to shoulder of 20 to 24 inches (51 to 61 cm), weight 50 to 80 pounds (22 to 36.2 kg).
Medium standard: height to shoulder of 17 to 20 inches (43 to 51 cm), weight 40 to 50 pounds (18 to 22 kg).
Miniature: height to shoulder of up to 20 inches (51 cm), weight 15 to 35 pounds (7 to 16 kg).

Colors

Goldendoodles are usually golden in color but with variations including white, cream, red, apricot, copper, gray, and black. Most Goldendoodles have white feathering. Some Goldendoodles will lighten in color as they age.

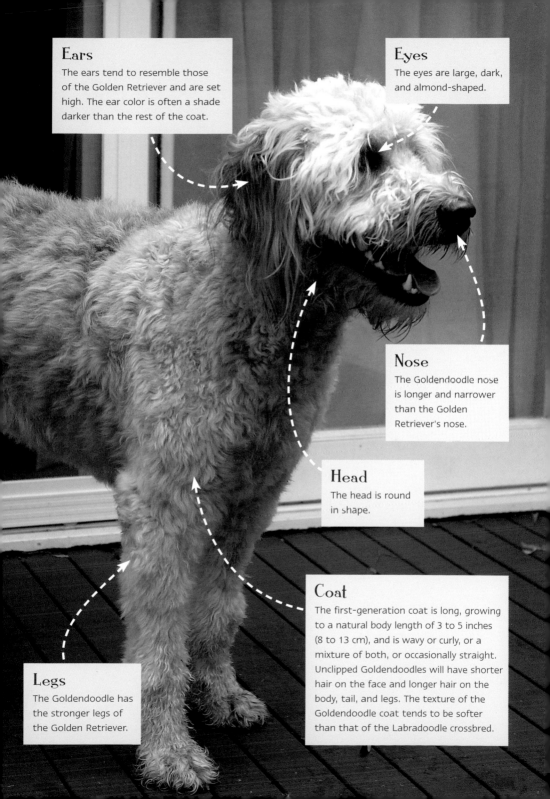

Ears
The ears tend to resemble those of the Golden Retriever and are set high. The ear color is often a shade darker than the rest of the coat.

Eyes
The eyes are large, dark, and almond-shaped.

Nose
The Goldendoodle nose is longer and narrower than the Golden Retriever's nose.

Head
The head is round in shape.

Legs
The Goldendoodle has the stronger legs of the Golden Retriever.

Coat
The first-generation coat is long, growing to a natural body length of 3 to 5 inches (8 to 13 cm), and is wavy or curly, or a mixture of both, or occasionally straight. Unclipped Goldendoodles will have shorter hair on the face and longer hair on the body, tail, and legs. The texture of the Goldendoodle coat tends to be softer than that of the Labradoodle crossbred.

Living with your Goldendoodle

Goldendoodles are frequently described as "gentle." They are said to have both intelligence and a sunny disposition. Because of their desire to please, Goldendoodles make good family pets.

General behavior
Goldendoodle owners report that their dogs are affectionate, loyal, and outgoing.

Activity levels
Goldendoodles require a moderate amount of daily exercise. They especially enjoy retrieving games. As both parent breeds are water dogs, Goldendoodles love the water.

Barking
Most Goldendoodles are quiet dogs as they have no protective or watchdog tendencies. The pitch of the bark varies with the size of the dog.

Temperament
Goldendoodles are gentle by nature and love to be with people. The temperament of a dog is directly related to parentage, so discrepancies can exist with any crossbred dog.

Other pets
Goldendoodles are generally good with other pets.

Children
Goldendoodles generally get on well with children but, as with all dogs, supervision and training are recommended.

Trainability
Goldendoodles are intelligent and eager to please so they are easy to train.

Working

Goldendoodles have shown good potential as working dogs. They are sometimes used as guide dogs, sniffer dogs, service dogs, and therapy dogs. A low-shedding coat provides an advantage when working with people. The first Goldendoodle Seeing Eye dog was trained at Guide Dogs of America (city of Los Angeles). Miniature Goldendoodles are now working as hearing dogs. Goldendoodles have also displayed an aptitude for work as sniffer dogs and have taken part in several studies in the United States. (See Working Dogs feature on page 54.)

VET'S ADVICE

Careful exercise

As with all larger dogs, take care with overexercising Goldendoodle puppies as this can lead to problems with the joints in fast-growing dogs. Also, do not exercise dogs right after a large meal as this can predispose them to bloating.

General health and lifespan

The average lifespan for a Goldendoodle is approximately 10 to 15 years, but parentage is one factor that will influence longevity.

Health problems include congenital heart disease, progressive retinal atrophy (PRA), patellar luxation (a knee problem), hip dysplasia, elbow dysplasia, allergies, Von Willebrand's disease, and hypothyroidism.

Ear infections may be a problem with (F1B) Goldendoodles that favor the Poodle. Plucking and cleaning the ear canal will help to reduce the incidence of ear infections. Eye problems are also common, especially if the hair or extraneous eyelashes get near the eyes.

Space needs

Goldendoodles vary in sizes but medium-sized dogs will adapt to an average backyard or garden.

Grooming

First-generation Goldendoodles are light to nonshedding. The coat is moderate to high maintenance and requires combing every few weeks. Owners often choose to cut back the fur every few months to make the coat easier to maintain. Backcrossed (F1B) Goldendoodles usually have a more Poodle-like, low-shedding coat; however, this means that they may need regular clipping.

Ears need to be kept clean and care needs to be taken of hair near the eyes.

The Pekapoo

Name variations: *Peekapoo, Pekepoo, Pekeapoo, Peke-a-poo*

Pekapoos are one of the older Poodle crossbreds. A compact dog with attractive markings, the Pekapoo is a cross between a Pekingese and a Miniature or Toy Poodle.

History of the Pekapoo

Pekapoos have been bred in the United States since the 1950s. Smaller than Cockapoos, Pekapoos gained a following at about the same time.

The Pekapoo remains popular in North America with dog owners seeking a small, healthy Poodle cross. Because of the Poodle genes, the first-generation Pekapoo may not have some of the health problems associated with purebred Pekingese and usually inherits a low-shedding, low-dander coat from the Poodle parent.

Recognition of breed

There is no official breed standard for the Pekapoo. Pekapoo breeders usually provide first-generation crosses.

Characteristics of the parent breeds

The first-generation Pekapoo usually inherits the low-shedding, low-dander coat associated with Poodles. This makes the Pekapoo a potentially good option for allergy sufferers.

The Poodle genes may also help improve those health problems of the Pekingese caused by the brachycephalic head (a short, broad, almost spherical head with a pushed-in muzzle). As Pekapoos have the longer snout of the Poodle, they find breathing easier. They also have a deeper socket for the eyeballs so the eyes are less likely to pop out than are the eyes of the Pekingese parent breed.

As both parent breeds are small dogs, the Pekapoo is tiny and makes an ideal lapdog.

First-generation (F1) Pekapoos

Pekapoos are first-generation crosses (the direct offspring of a Toy or Miniature Poodle and a Pekingese). Either breed can be the sire or dam but the Pekingese is usually the dam.

Multi-generation Pekapoos

The Pekapoo has not been developed as a multi-generation crossbred. Second- or

ABOVE First-generation black Pekapoo puppy.

ABOVE First-generation adult Pekapoo with similar coloring to the Pekingese parent breed.

third-generation dogs would be more likely to have the health problems that the first cross is intended to avoid.

Crossbreeding goals

The Pekapoo is intended to be a small, healthy companion dog. This cross suits many people, especially the elderly, who are looking for a small, easily-managed dog with potentially fewer health problems than the Pekingese and a coat that sheds less.

Choosing a breeder

You may be able to locate reputable breeders of Pekapoos by asking breeders of other Poodle crossbreds.

A reputable breeder will use good breeding stock and select parents on the basis of temperament as well as looks and genetic soundness. The breeder should also provide proof that the puppy's parents were screened for inherited diseases.

Screening tests

Breeders should screen for luxating patellas, hip dysplasia, Legg-Calvé-Perthes disease, and eye diseases. (See pages 124 to 125 for more information about screening tests.)

Appearance

Tail
The Pekapoo has a plumed tail.

Pekapoo characteristics
There is no official breed standard for the Pekapoo. The following are characteristics of a typical first-generation (F1) Pekapoo.

General appearance
The breeds mixed will produce varying results.

Size ranges
Pekapoo sizes vary so their height to shoulder can be up to 11 inches (28 cm) and weight can be somewhere between 4 and 20 pounds (1.8 and 9 kg).

Colors
Pekapoos can be any color that comes from the Poodle or the Pekingese. These include white, silver, sable, cream, buff, apricot, red, chocolate, and black, as well as phantom (black with tan markings).

Legs
The Pekapoo legs are longer than the legs of the Pekingese.

Eyes
The eyes of the Pekapoo are more deeply set than those of the Pekingese.

Ears
Darker markings on the ears of the Pekapoo may result from the Pekingese parent breed.

Mouth
One possible trait is an underbite.

Coat
The coat is open with wavy texture and low to medium shedding.

Living with your Pekapoo

Pekapoos are intelligent family dogs that are happy to be petted and make excellent lapdogs.

General behavior
Pekapoo owners report that their dogs are protective and affectionate with their family but can be wary of strangers. Pekapoos prefer to be with people and share in their owners' lives. They are not suited to being left in the backyard.

Activity levels
Pekapoos are active dogs that will enjoy regular walking and games. However, Pekapoos should not be overexercised and special care needs to be taken in hot weather. They are prone to heatstroke because any breathing difficulties make it hard for them to lose heat via panting.

Barking
The Pekapoo likes to bark.

Temperament
Pekapoos are friendly dogs. The temperament of a dog is directly related to parentage, so discrepancies can exist with any crossbred dog.

Other pets
Pekapoos usually get along well with other dogs and with cats if introduced to them from an early age.

Children
If they are introduced to children early on, Pekapoos will be sociable and nonaggressive. However, as with all dogs, supervision and training are recommended. As Pekapoos are quite small they can be hurt easily and may require protection from young children.

Trainability

Pekapoos are moderately easy to train.

Working

Pekapoos may be suitable as therapy dogs. Low-shedding coats provide an advantage when working with people.

General health and lifespan

The average lifespan for a Pekapoo is about 10 to 15 years but parentage is one factor that will influence longevity.

Health problems may include progressive retinal atrophy, Legg-Calvé-Perthes disease

(a genetic hip-joint disease) and hip dysplasia. Both parent breeds experience medial luxating kneecaps (patellas), which is relatively common.

Many toy breeds, especially Pekingese and Poodles, are prone to collapsing windpipes where the tracheal cartilages collapse episodically, causing a constriction of the airways. Pekapoos may experience breathing problems and be prone to heatstroke.

Space needs

Pekapoos can be happily active indoors and may be fine without a backyard or garden. They enjoy walking and games in safe open spaces.

Grooming

Pekapoos are low to average shedders. The Pekapoo coat should be combed and brushed approximately twice a week. Coats may be trimmed or kept long. A coat that is kept long will require more frequent brushing to prevent matting. Owners may prefer to clip the coat in the summer months. The eyes, ears, nose, and facial folds need to be kept clean. Hair in the ear canal may need to be plucked.

The Shepadoodle

Name variations: *Shepapoo*

The crossbreeding of a herding dog with a Poodle is a relatively new approach. The Shepadoodle is an energetic mix of the German Shepherd with the Standard or Miniature Poodle.

History of the Shepadoodle

With growing public awareness of the low-shedding Poodle crosses it was inevitable that people would look to another popular dog like the German Shepherd to produce a dynamic new crossbred.

Shepadoodles have only been bred in America and Canada since around 2001 so breeding programs are still in the early stages.

Recognition of breed

There is no official breed standard for the Shepadoodle. Most breeders provide first-generation crosses.

Characteristics of the parent breeds

The first-generation Shepadoodle is likely to inherit a moderately shedding coat because of the Poodle parent breed.

Shepadoodles tend to be more like a German Shepherd than a Poodle and inherit both the energy and the herding, protective nature of the Shepherd. The German Shepherd parent breed is a herding dog that was bred with an instinct to patrol a boundary and, for example, restrict a flock of sheep from entering or leaving the area within the boundary. This "tending" style

of herding instinct makes the German Shepherd an excellent guard dog and this instinct may also be inherited by the Shepadoodle.

Shepadoodles are intelligent, like both parent breeds, and sociable, like the Poodle.

Initially popular with families wanting a larger Poodle cross, Shepadoodles now come in medium and miniature sizes.

First-generation (F1) Shepadoodles

Standard Shepadoodles are first-generation crosses (the direct offspring of a Standard Poodle and German Shepherd); either breed can be the sire or dam, depending on relative sizes. Miniature Shepadoodles are the first-generation cross of a Miniature or Toy Poodle with a German Shepherd; the German Shepherd is the dam.

ABOVE First-generation Shepadoodle puppy with white coat.

FACING PAGE First-generation adult Standard Shepadoodle.

Multi-generation Shepadoodles

Some breeders have developed backcrossed (F1B) Shepadoodles to improve the chance of a low-shedding Poodle-like coat.

Crossbreeding goals

German Shepherds are big shedders. The Shepadoodle offers the personality traits of the German Shepherd, but with the benefits of a moderately shedding coat.

Shepadoodles have been bred as a family dog but some may inherit the herding instincts of the Shepherd parent breed and have a future as working dogs.

Choosing a breeder

The Shepadoodle is a relatively new crossbred but you may be able to locate reputable breeders of Shepadoodles by asking breeders of other Poodle crossbreds.

A reputable breeder will use good breeding stock and select parents on the basis of temperament as well as looks and genetic soundness. The breeder should also provide proof that the puppy's parents were screened for inherited diseases.

Screening tests

Because the German Shepherd parent breed is predisposed to many problematic traits, it is important that you ask about screening for inherited diseases before purchasing a Shepadoodle puppy.

Breeders should screen for hip dysplasia and eye diseases. (See pages 124 to 125 for more information about screening tests.)

CHAPTER 7

 # Appearance

Shepadoodle characteristics
There is no official breed standard for the Shepadoodle. The following are characteristics of a typical first-generation Shepadoodle (picture shows a closely clipped dog).

General appearance
The Shepadoodle tends to look more like the German Shepherd (and is sometimes mistaken for an Irish Wolfhound).

Tail
The tail is long and saber-like with the hair swirling around it, although not usually feathered.

Size ranges
A standard-sized Shepadoodle has a height to shoulder of 20 to 28 inches (51 to 71 cm) and would weigh around 50 to 90 pounds (22.6 to 40.8 kg).
Miniature Shepadoodles usually result in a medium-sized dog with a height to shoulder of 17 to 20 inches (43 to 51 cm) and weight of about 20 to 50 pounds (9 to 22.6 kg).

Colors
Colors can include solid black, chalk, cream, apricot, chocolate, silver, blue, combination black and white, brindle, and white markings. Some dogs can have tan markings provided there are phantom poodles in the bloodline.

Coat
The first-generation coat is wavy or curly with a wiry texture and can have a somewhat scruffy look when left unclipped. Backcrossed Shepadoodles (F1B) may have a fleece coat.

e n

Build
The Shepadoodle is a sturdy dog.

Ears
Shepadoodle usually have folded ears rather than the pricked-up ears of the German Shepherd.

Eyes
The eyes are dark in color.

Nose
The snout of the Shepadoodle is similar to the Labradoodle crossbred but longer and more narrow.

Legs
Shepadoodle legs are long and more like the German Shepherd legs.

Living with your Shepadoodle

Shepadoodles are intelligent, fun-loving, and protective. Owners report that they have a great disposition and make superb companions.

General behavior
Shepadoodle owners describe their dogs as energetic, highly intelligent, and loyal.

Activity levels
Shepadoodles are athletic, lively dogs and they require daily exercise.

Barking
Shepadoodles may bark as watchdogs but tend to be quiet dogs if the parent is not a barker.

Temperament
Shepadoodles are energetic and free-spirited. Breeders report that they are nonaggressive and calm, even as puppies. They are sociable and enjoy the company of people. Shepadoodles can become very attached to their human companions, following them around and behaving protectively. They may show signs of the herding instinct from the German Shepherd parent breed and closely watch, nip, or try to direct family members as they go for walks.

The temperament of a dog is directly related to parentage, so discrepancies can exist with any crossbred dog.

Other pets
Shepadoodles are generally good with other pets. Owners report that Shepadoodle puppies will follow larger animals.

Children
Shepadoodles are generally good with children but, as with all dogs, supervision and training are recommended.

VET'S ADVICE

Temperament
Temperament must be adequately assessed before crossbreeding. German Shepherds are generally good-natured but occasionally suffer from neurotic and fear aggression behavior as well as being destructive when left alone for long periods of time. There may be problems with the Shepadoodle offspring if a female German Shepherd with a significant potential for neuroses is crossed with a male miniature Poodle with similar traits such as anxiety and hyperactivity. Due to this and extreme size differences, the male German Shepherd and female Standard Poodle may be the best combination.

Trainability

Both German Shepherds and Poodles are intelligent dogs, and the Shepadoodle offspring are extremely smart, eager to learn, and easy to train.

Working

Shepadoodles have really been developed as moderately shedding family pets but breeders report that those with the herding instinct may have potential as working dogs on farms. The crossbred is very new, so Shepadoodles have yet to be assessed for herding work or used in a working environment. Their protective instinct provides potential for them to work in different roles. Some Shepadoodles are being trained as therapy dogs.

General health and lifespan

The average lifespan for a Shepadoodle would be approximately 12 to 15 years, but parentage is one factor that will influence longevity.

Health problems include genetic problems that affect both parent breeds such as hip dysplasia and eye disease.

Space needs

Shepadoodles can be content in the house but need lots of exercise. They would do better in a large backyard or garden. The smaller crossbred offspring from miniature parents may require less space.

Grooming

First-generation Shepadoodles have a curly or wavy coat and are usually moderate shedders. They require occasional grooming and an optional haircut once or twice a year. It is difficult to determine the Shepadoodle grooming requirements before they shed their puppy coats at the age of about eight months.

The Aussiedoodle

Name variations: *Aussiepoo*

A new herding dog hybrid, the Aussiedoodle is the distinctive cross between the Standard or Miniature Australian Shepherd and the Standard, Miniature, or Toy Poodle.

History of the Aussiedoodle

The Aussiedoodle crossbred has been developed only in the past few years. Like the Shepadoodle, the Aussiedoodle combines a Poodle and a herding dog. The Aussiedoodle also features unusual coat colorings.

Aussiedoodles, like their Australian Shepherd parent breed (which originated in the 1960s as a herding dog on American ranches), are actually more popular in North America than they are in Australia.

Recognition of breed

There is no official breed standard for the Aussiedoodle. Most breeders provide first-generation crosses.

Characteristics of the parent breeds

The Aussiedoodle may inherit the low-shedding, low-dander coat associated with Poodles. This makes the Aussiedoodle a potentially good option for allergy sufferers.

Aussiedoodles may also inherit the intelligence and sociability of the Poodle.

The Australian Shepherd parent breed is known for its attractive coat colors such as black, blue merle (a marbling of gray and

black), red (ranging from light cinnamon to liver), and red merle (marbling of red and silver or buff), and also white and tan markings on the face, chest, front, and rear legs. Aussiedoodles share the distinctive coloring of the Australian Shepherd parent breed. The blue eyes associated with some Australian Shepherds won't appear in first-generation Aussiedoodles although occasionally some will have partially blue eyes. Second-generation blue merle Aussiedoodles may have blue or partially blue eyes.

Crossbreeding with a solid or parti colored dog like the Poodle means that the first-generation Aussiedoodle avoids the health problems that sometimes arise in the offspring of "Double Merle" matings of the Australian Shepherd parent breeds.

The Australian Shepherd parent breed is a versatile herding dog that was bred to control all kinds of livestock but especially cattle. Associated with a "driving" style of herding

ABOVE Black and white Miniature Aussiedoodle puppy.

livestock, Australian Shepherds are used for work such as moving stock into a group and directing the group to new grazing land. Aussiedoodle breeding programs are relatively new but breeders report that this cross may inherit the herding instinct of the Australian Shepherd parent.

First-generation (F1) Aussiedoodles

Standard Aussiedoodles are first-generation crosses of a Standard Poodle and an Australian Shepherd. Either breed can be the dam. Miniature and Toy Aussiedoodles are the first-generation cross of a Miniature or Toy Poodle with a Miniature Australian Shepherd. The Australian Shepherd is the dam.

Multi-generation Aussiedoodles

Some breeders have developed second generation dogs.

Crossbreeding goals

Australian Shepherds are big shedders, so Aussiedoodles that inherit the low-shedding, low-dander coat of the Poodle provide a potentially good option for allergy sufferers. Aussiedoodle breeders also aim to retain the gorgeous coloring of the Australian Shepherd. Crosses that inherit the herding instinct of the Australian Shepherd may have uses as working dogs in the future.

Choosing a breeder

The Aussiedoodle is a very recent crossbred but you may be able to locate reputable breeders of Aussiedoodles by asking breeders of other Poodle crossbreds. If conducting Internet searches on the Aussiedoodle, note that some breeders call the Australian Cattle Dog x Poodle cross an Aussiedoodle, so make

ABOVE Standard Aussiedoodle adult dog.

sure the breeder is providing the particular cross you seek.

A reputable breeder will use good breeding stock and select parents on the basis of temperament as well as looks and genetic soundness. The breeder should also provide proof that the puppy's parents were screened for inherited diseases.

Screening tests

Breeders should screen for hip dysplasia and eye diseases. (See pages 124 to 125 for more information about screening tests.)

Appearance

Aussiedoodle characteristics

There is no official breed standard for the Aussiedoodle. The following are characteristics of a typical first-generation Aussiedoodle.

General appearance

The Aussiedoodle resembles both the Poodle and Australian Shepherd parent breeds.

Tail

The tail of the Aussiedoodle is long and feathered and is sometimes overcurled.

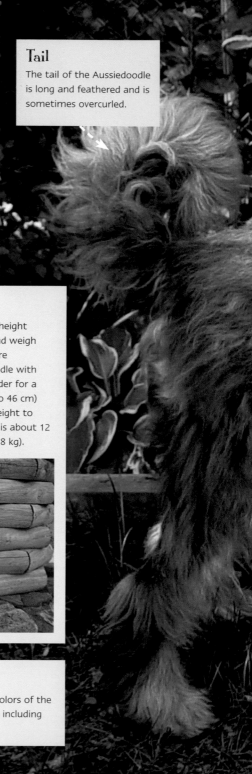

Size ranges

A medium- to large-sized Aussiedoodle could have a height to shoulder of about 20 to 30 inches (51 to 76 cm) and weigh between 25 and 50 pounds (11 and 22.6 kg). Miniature Aussiedoodles are the cross of a Miniature or Toy Poodle with a Miniature Australian Shepherd. The height to shoulder for a Miniature Aussiedoodle is about 13 to 18 inches (33 to 46 cm) and weight is 15 to 30 pounds (6.8 to 13.6 kg). The height to shoulder for the recently developed Toy Aussiedoodle is about 12 inches (31 cm) and weight is 6 to 15 pounds (2.7 to 6.8 kg).

Colors

Aussiedoodle puppies often retain the merle and tri-colors of the Australian Shepherd. They come in a variety of colors, including blue merle, black, red merle, and red.

Eyes
The eyes of the Aussiedoodle are usually brown. Partially blue eyes are occasionally seen in first-generation blue merle Aussiedoodles.

Mouth
Aussiedoodle muzzles are usually more square in shape than the muzzles of the Australian Shepherd parent breed.

Coat
The coat length is generally moderate, can be straight or slightly wavy, and appears shaggy but has a soft, silky texture.

Legs
Aussiedoodle legs are usually longer than that of the Australian Shepherd parent breed.

Living with your Aussiedoodle

Aussiedoodles are intelligent dogs that enjoy human company and make great family dogs.

General behavior
Aussiedoodle owners describe their dogs as active, devoted, and extremely intelligent. They are happy to stay near the family but will also be relaxed by themselves.

Activity levels
Aussiedoodles are lively dogs and daily exercise is essential. Aussiedoodles love exercise and breeders report that they are energetic without being hyper and would be good in agility.

Barking
Aussiedoodles can be barkers if not trained properly, but are not "yappy" dogs.

Temperament
Aussiedoodles are energetic, enthusiastic, smart, and attentive to their owners.

As Aussiedoodles are very loyal family dogs and can be leery of strangers and reserved, it is recommended that owners socialize their puppies with other dogs, people, and new places and things. This makes them more confident and less easily intimidated. Socialization is important for all dogs, but very important for Aussiedoodles.

The temperament of a dog is directly related to parentage, so discrepancies can exist with any crossbred dog.

Deafness and the merle coat

Deafness can be inherited by some of the offspring of two Australian Shepherds with the merle coat gene. The double merle offspring with a predominantly white coat (with some merle patches) can suffer deafness and other problems. Luckily, the double merle potential problems are not an issue in the first-generation Aussiedoodle as one parent (the Poodle) has a solid or parti coat. Deafness could be an issue if a merled Aussiedoodle is then backcrossed to a merle Australian Shepherd, but breeders report that they avoid this double merle combination. Dogs with a merled coat are often much sought after, so when seeking a merled puppy contact a reputable Aussiedoodle breeder who will provide first-generation crosses and supply details on the puppies' parentage and the steps taken to avoid inherited deafness.

Other pets

Aussiedoodles are generally good with other pets. Breeders recommend that owners take the time to introduce the Aussiedoodle to other dogs and to other pets.

Children

Aussiedoodles are generally good with children but, as with all dogs, supervision and training are recommended.

Trainability

Australian Shepherds are intelligent dogs, as are Poodles.

The parents' intelligence means that Aussiedoodles learn quickly and are easy to house-train. Breeders also report that Aussiedoodles need to be trained and to receive boundaries because of their high intelligence. This makes the Aussiedoodle more suited to owners who are committed to providing training.

Working

Aussiedoodles have really been developed as low-shedding, low-dander family pets, but breeders report that those with the herding instinct may have potential as working dogs on farms. The crossbred is very new, so the Aussiedoodle has yet to be assessed for herding work or used in a working environment.

General health and lifespan

The average lifespan for an Aussiedoodle would be approximately 12 to 15 years but parentage is one factor that will influence longevity.

Health problems include genetic problems that affect both parent breeds such as eye diseases and hip dysplasia. Hip dysplasia can affect both the Miniature Australian Shepherd and Miniature or Toy Poodle (although it is

less common), as well as the standard-sized parent breeds, so all sizes of Aussiedoodles can be affected by this condition.

Aussiedoodles can have hair in their ears, like the Poodle, so when groomed the hairs need to be pulled and the ears require regular checking and cleaning.

"Merle" is a pattern gene that dilutes dark coat colors, usually in a splotchy pattern, and it is seen in the Australian Shepherd parent breed. Merle to merle matings are not recommended as they sometimes produce mostly white pups that can suffer from deafness or blindness. Fortunately, the first-generation Aussiedoodle avoids this because at least one parent (the Poodle) has a solid or parti coat.

Space needs

Aussiedoodles can be content in the house but need lots of exercise. They would do better in a large backyard or garden. Miniature Aussiedoodles may require less space.

Grooming

First-generation Aussiedoodles often have a low-shedding, low-dander coat. The texture is soft and silky and the coat is relatively easy to maintain. Owners may choose to use a poodle clip on the Aussiedoodle, giving them a "merled" poodle appearance that is quite different to the natural shaggy look. When grooming, have the hair in the ears pulled to reduce the chances of infection.

Other popular Poodle crosses

Poodle x Bichon Frise	Poochon
Poodle x Cavalier King Charles	Cavoodle/Cavapoo
Poodle x Chihuahua	Wapoo
Poodle x Collie	Cadoodle
Poodle x Lhasa Apso	Lhasa-Poo
Poodle x Pomeranian	Pooranian
Poodle x Scottish Terrier	Scoodle
Poodle x Shih Tzu	Shih-Poo
Poodle x Silky Terrier	Poolky
Poodle x Toy Fox Terrier	Foodle

The Yorkiepoo

Name variations: *Yorkipoo*

The Yorkiepoo, one of the smaller Poodle crossbred companion dogs, is the lively cross between a Yorkshire Terrier and a Toy or Miniature Poodle.

History of the Yorkiepoo

Yorkiepoos became popular Poodle crossbreds in the last decade, as another potentially low-shedding, low-dander dog combining a small size with very appealing features. Yorkiepoos are mostly popular in the United States.

Recognition of crossbreed

There is no official breed standard for the Yorkiepoo. An organization based in the United States, <www.yorkiepoo.org>, gives a description of the aims of Yorkiepoo breeders.

ABOVE Adult first generation Yorkiepoo.

Characteristics of the parent breeds

Yorkiepoos usually inherit the low-shedding, low-dander coat associated with the Poodle, making them a potentially good option for allergy sufferers.

Yorkiepoos are smart, curious dogs, ideally possessing the intelligence of the Poodle and the determination and resilience of the Yorkshire Terrier.

First-generation (F1) Yorkiepoos

Yorkiepoos are usually first-generation crosses of a Toy or Miniature Poodle and a Yorkshire Terrier. The dam should always be the bigger of the two parent breeds to avoid puppies becoming too large and complicating the delivery for the mother.

Multi-generation Yorkiepoos

The Yorkiepoo has not yet been developed as a multi-generation crossbred.

Crossbreeding goals

The Yorkiepoo has been bred as a companion dog. The low-shedding, low-dander coat of the Poodle makes the crossbred a potentially useful dog for allergy sufferers.

The compact size of both the parent breeds ensures that, despite variations, the Yorkiepoo offspring are likely to be small, and many are tiny.

The goal of crossbreeding the Poodle and Yorkshire Terrier is to produce a healthy, happy toy dog with fewer genetic problems than the parent breeds and a soft, silky low-shedding coat.

Choosing a breeder

Locate reputable Yorkiepoo breeders by asking breeders of other Poodle crossbreds. The organization <www.yorkiepoo.org> may also provide advice on locating breeders.

A reputable breeder will use good breeding stock and select parents on the basis of temperament as well as looks and genetic soundness. The breeder should also provide proof that the puppy's parents were screened for inherited diseases.

ABOVE Yorkiepoo litter showing range of colors and markings.

Screening tests

Breeders of Yorkiepoos should screen for eye diseases, luxating patellas, hip dysplasia, and Legg-Calvé-Perthes disease. (See pages 124 to 125 for more information about screening tests.)

Other popular Yorkshire Terrier crosses

Yorkshire Terrier x Bichon Frise	Yorkiechon/Yo-Chon
Yorkshire Terrier x Chihuahua	Chorkie
Yorkshire Terrier x Lhasa Apso	Yorkie-Apso
Yorkshire Terrier x Maltese	Malkie
Yorkshire Terrier x Pekingese	Yorkinese
Yorkshire Terrier x Pomeranian	Yoranian
Yorkshire Terrier x Pug	Pugshire

Appearance

Yorkiepoo characteristics
There is no official breed standard for the Yorkiepoo. Yorkiepoo.org offers these guidelines on the characteristics of a first-generation Yorkiepoo.

General appearance
The impression one should get from a Yorkiepoo is that of a well-proportioned dog.

Tail
The tail is usually high set.

Size ranges
The Yorkiepoo's mature weight will range from 3 to 14 pounds (1.3 to 6.3 kg) and its height will range from 7 to 15 inches (18 to 38 cm), depending on the size of the parent.

Colors
The coat comes in all different colors and usually a mix of colors is involved. Colors can include white, sable, silver, cream, apricot, tan, red, chocolate, gray, and black.

Ears
The ears may stand up like a Yorkshire Terrier's or may drop like a Poodle's.

Eyes
Eyes are dark with a lively expression. They can be almond-shaped or round.

Nose
The nose is black.

Coat
The coat should be soft and silky and the fur can be wavy, curly, or straight.

Feet
The feet are small and oval-shaped.

Living with your Yorkiepoo

Yorkiepoos are small dogs with big personalities.

General behavior
Yorkiepoos are described as friendly, curious, lively, self-confident, playful, watchful, and loving.

Activity levels
Yorkiepoos are energetic dogs. They are agile and can jump high and run very fast. They appreciate regular walks and playing in safe open spaces.

Barking
Yorkiepoos like to bark.

Temperament
Yorkiepoos are happy and fun-loving dogs. They love people and dislike being excluded from family activities. Yorkiepoos are intelligent and easily trained but they can display stubbornness. They make excellent watchdogs.

The temperament of a dog is directly related to parentage, so discrepancies can exist with any crossbred dog.

Other pets
Yorkiepoos are generally good with other pets.

Children
Yorkiepoos are generally good with children but, as with all dogs, supervision and training are recommended.

As Yorkiepoos are very small dogs, they can be easily hurt and may require protection from young children.

Trainability
Yorkiepoos are intelligent and they learn tricks easily if rewarded with treats.

Working
Yorkiepoos may be used as therapy dogs. Their small size makes them suitable for contact with the elderly. A low-shedding,

low-dander coat may also provide an advantage when working with people.

General health and lifespan

The average lifespan for a Yorkiepoo is about 10 to 15 years but parentage is one factor that will influence a dog's longevity.

Health problems experienced by Yorkiepoos include liver shunts, epilepsy, common skin diseases, eye problems, patellar luxation (a knee problem), hip dysplasia, and Legg-Calvé-Perthes disease (a genetic hip-joint disease). "Porto systemic shunts" are a rare but well-documented inherited disorder. Yorkshire Terriers are prone to tooth decay, but this is less likely in the Yorkiepoo. As Yorkiepoos age, endocrine disorders, especially hypothyroidism and Cushings disease, are possible problems.

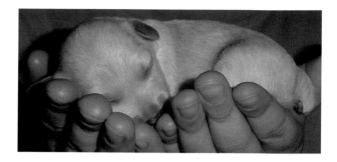

VET'S ADVICE

Shunts

Congenital shunts are seen in some larger breeds and many small-breed dogs, such as Yorkshire Terriers or Toy Poodles, so shunts could affect the Yorkiepoo. Portosystemic shunts pose a serious health problem to dogs. Shunts are an abnormality of the vessels where blood is diverted away from the liver, allowing toxins to circulate through the body. Shunts can be congenital or acquired and be present (in single or multiple form) inside or outside the liver. Dogs with congenital shunts tend to be small for their age and breed. Other signs of shunts include excessive drinking and frequent urination. A vet will first check blood and urine samples. Treatment may include surgery or a specially prescribed diet and medications.

Space needs

Yorkiepoos can live in a house or an apartment, as they are active indoors.

Grooming

Yorkiepoos usually have a low-shedding, low-dander coat. They require daily brushing and combing to prevent the coat from matting. They also need regular clipping. Regular bathing, ear cleaning, and possible plucking are recommended. Any hair growing into the eyes needs to be clipped to prevent irritation. As with the Yorkshire Terrier, as long as you brush or comb the hair to grow downward, it will grow away from the eyes. If you clip it away from the eyes, then it will always grow into the eyes and you will have to keep clipping it on a regular basis.

The Maltepoo

Name variations: *Maltapoo, Moodle, Malti-poo, Maltipoo, Malta-poo*

Poodle crossbreeders have developed many small companion dogs with low-shedding, low-dander coats. One such dog with wide appeal is the fun-loving Maltepoo, a Maltese crossed with a Toy or Miniature Poodle.

History of the Maltepoo

Maltepoos became widely known in the last decade and this diminutive crossbred now has a high public profile. Maltepoos have enjoyed the spotlight through their association with designer dog—and designer handbag—toting celebrity owners. Maltepoos (also known as Moodles) are popular lapdogs in the United States, Canada, and Australia.

Recognition of breeds

There is no official breed standard for the Maltepoo. The North American Maltepoo/Maltipoo Club and Registry (NAMCR) provides a description of the crossbred and guidelines for accepted crossbreeding of first-generation and second-generation Maltepoos.

Characteristics of the parent breeds

The Maltepoo usually inherits the woolly, low-shedding, low-dander coat associated with Poodles, making this cross a potentially good option for allergy sufferers. Maltepoos are said to be smart dogs, like the Poodle parent breed. The Maltese is a friendly, healthy toy dog and the Maltepoo shares these qualities.

Like both parent breeds, Maltepoos are usually small dogs and many of them are tiny.

First-generation (F1) Maltepoos

Maltepoos are usually first-generation crosses of a Toy or Miniature Poodle and a Maltese. Either breed can be the sire or the dam.

Multi-generation Maltepoos

Multi-generation Maltepoos have been bred in the United States, according to NAMCR. The second-generation (F2) dogs are more likely to favor one of the parent breeds. NAMCR's guidelines state that only (F2) Maltepoos can be used to breed third-generation (F3) dogs.

Crossbreeding goals

Maltepoo breeders have focused on producing a small, healthy, low-shedding family dog.

Choosing a breeder

Locate reputable Maltepoo breeders by asking breeders of other Poodle crossbreds. NAMCR,

ABOVE First-generation Maltepoo puppy with all-white coat.

ABOVE First-generation adult Maltepoo with black coat and white markings.

the Maltepoo association based in the United States, may give advice on locating breeders.

A reputable breeder will choose from good breeding stock and select parents on the basis of temperament as well as looks and genetic soundness. The breeder should also provide proof that the puppy's parents were screened for inherited diseases.

Screening tests

Breeders of Maltepoos should screen for eye diseases, luxating patellas, hip dysplasia, and Legg-Calvé-Perthes disease. (See pages 124 to 125 for more information about screening tests.)

Other popular Maltese crosses

Maltese x Bichon Frise	Maltichon
Maltese x Cavalier King Charles Spaniel	Maltalier/Cav-A-Malt
Maltese x Chihuahua	Malchi
Maltese x Papillon	Malton
Maltese x Pekingese	Peke-A-Tese
Maltese x Pomeranian	Maltapom/Pomanees

Appearance

Maltepoo characteristics
There is no official breed standard for the Maltepoo. A typical first-generation dog has the following characteristics.

General appearance
The Maltepoo resembles both the Poodle and Maltese parent breeds.

Tail
The tail of the Maltepoo is curled.

Size ranges
The size of a Maltepoo will vary depending on the parent breeds, but the height to shoulder can be as high as 14 inches (36 cm). The Maltepoo's mature weight is generally somewhere between 5 and 12 pounds (2.2 and 5.4 kg), but Maltepoos can weigh as much as 23 pounds (10 kg).

Colors
Maltepoos come in a variety of colors. Light colors (including white, silver, and cream) are more common, but Maltepoos can also have a black coat.

Legs
The Maltepoo's legs are usually short.

Ears
The ears are often shorter, like those of the Maltese parent breed.

Eyes
The eyes of the Maltepoo are often dark.

Nose
The nose of the Maltepoo is often dark.

Coat
The coat is woolly.

Living with your Maltepoo

Maltepoos are described as bouncy and outgoing dogs.

General behavior

Owners report that Maltepoos are feisty, cuddly, alert, gentle, loving balls of fun.

Activity levels

Maltepoos are active dogs that will enjoy going for walks. They like ball games and playing in safe open spaces.

Barking

Maltepoos like to bark.

Temperament

Maltepoos are loyal family dogs with an outgoing personality. However, temperament must be selected to avoid barking, aggression to strangers, dominance behavior with certain family members, and overt aggression around other dogs.

The temperament of a dog is directly related to parentage, so discrepancies can exist with any crossbred dog.

Other pets

Maltepoos are generally good with other pets.

Children

Maltepoos are generally good with children but, as with all dogs, supervision and training are recommended. Maltepoos are sometimes very small and can be easily hurt, so may need protection from young children.

Trainability

Maltepoos are bright and easy to train.

Working

Maltepoos may be used as therapy dogs. Their small size makes them suitable for contact with the elderly. A low-shedding, low-dander coat may also provide an advantage when working with people.

General health and lifespan

The average lifespan for a Maltepoo is about 10 to 15 years but parentage is one factor that will influence longevity.

Health problems experienced by Maltepoos could include liver shunts, epilepsy, common skin diseases, eye problems, patellar luxation, hip dysplasia, and Legg-Calvé-Perthes disease. "Porto systemic shunts" is a rare but well-documented inherited disorder that may occur. As the Maltepoo ages, endocrine disorders, especially hypothyroidism and Cushings disease, are common.

Maltese breeds often get "White Shaker Syndrome," a poorly understood neurological disease seen commonly in little white dogs like the Maltese. Maltepoos, being crossbred dogs, are less likely to have White Shaker Syndrome.

Space needs

Maltepoos can live in a house or an apartment, as they are active dogs when indoors.

VET'S ADVICE

Eye problems

Maltese and Poodles both suffer from PRA (Progressive Retinal Atrophy), an inherited disorder where the retina becomes progressively atrophied and eventually causes blindness, so this may be a problem with the Maltepoo crossbred. Retinal detachment and dysplasia is another inherited problem that may affect the Maltepoo. More common in the Maltepoo would be problems such as distichiasis and trichiasis (abnormal eyelashes or rows of eyelashes), which irritate the eye. If your dog shows signs of distichiasis and trichiasis, consult your veterinarian. Treatment may warrant eyelash removal by lasering, surgery, or other methods. Cataracts may develop as the Maltepoo ages.

Grooming

First-generation Maltepoos are usually low-shedding dogs. They require daily brushing and combing to prevent the coat from matting. They also need regular clipping. For a clipped look some owners will clip the face every month. The body can be clipped every year or two. Regular bathing, ear cleaning, and possible plucking are recommended.

The Maltese Shih Tzu

Name variations: *Mal-Shi, Malt-Tzu, Maltzu, Malti zu*

Unusually, the playful Maltese Shih Tzu is known by the name of its cross and has been able to gain acceptance and great popularity without the addition of a widely used "cute" name. The Maltese Shih Tzu combines two low-shedding, low-dander companion dog parent breeds: the appealing Maltese and the distinguished looking Shih Tzu.

History of the Maltese Shih Tzu

The Maltese Shih Tzu was actively developed by Australian breeders during the 1990s and is now one of the most popular dogs in Australia. The Maltese Shih Tzu develops into a friendly, outgoing dog. This cross may also avoid the health problems associated with the nose and eyes of the Shih Tzu. Popular with pet owners young and old looking for a clean, easily managed lapdog, the Maltese Shih Tzu is also attracting a following in the United States.

Recognition of breed

There is no official breed standard for the Maltese Shih Tzu. Most breeders provide first generation crosses.

Characteristics of the parent breeds

The Shih Tzu parent breed has the large eyes and flattish face sometimes associated with eye and breathing problems. The Maltese Shih Tzu offspring usually have a longer muzzle than their Shih Tzu parent, because the Maltese parent breed has a pointy nose, so they should experience fewer of these eye and breathing problems.

The Maltese is an all-white dog and the Shih Tzu parent breed is multicolored, so the Maltese Shih Tzu offspring come in a range of colors, usually white, or a mix of brown, white, and black.

Both parent breeds have long, low-shedding, low-dander coats that Maltese Shih Tzus inherit. As a result, they may require lots of grooming to prevent matting.

First-generation (F1) Maltese Shih Tzus

Maltese Shih Tzus are the first-generation cross of a Maltese and a Shih Tzu. The Maltese is usually used as the dam because the Shih Tzu parent breed has difficulty whelping.

ABOVE First generation Maltese Shih Tzu puppy.

Multi-generation Maltese Shih Tzus

Some second-generation (F2) dogs have been bred, but the Maltese Shih Tzu has not been developed as a multi-generation crossbred.

Crossbreeding goals

The Maltese Shih Tzu has been bred as a playful, healthy companion dog. The low-shedding, low-dander coat makes this cross potentially useful for allergy sufferers.

Choosing a breeder

You may be able to locate reputable Maltese Shih Tzu breeders by asking breeders of other Maltese crossbreds.

ABOVE First-generation adult Maltese Shih Tzu featuring mostly white coat with buff markings.

A reputable breeder will use good breeding stock and select parents on the basis of temperament as well as looks and genetic soundness. The breeder should also provide proof that the puppy's parents were screened for inherited diseases.

Screening tests

Breeders of Maltese Shih Tzus should screen for eye diseases, and luxating patellas. (See pages 124 to 125 for more information about screening tests.)

Appearance

Maltese Shih Tzu characteristics

There is no official breed standard for the Maltese Shih Tzu. The following are characteristics of a first-generation Maltese Shih Tzu dog.

General appearance

Maltese Shih Tzus usually appear as a combination of both parent breeds.

Tail

The Maltese Shih Tzu tail is curled.

Size ranges

A standard Maltese Shih Tzu's height to shoulder ranges from about 10 to 20 inches (26 to 51 cm). The mature weight can be between 15 and 30 pounds (6.8 and 13.6 kg).

Colors

The Maltese Shih Tzu can come in the colors of the Shih Tzu, usually white or a mix of brown, white, and black.

Legs

The legs of the Maltese Shih Tzu are short.

Ears
Darker markings on the ears reflect the coloring of the Shih Tzu.

Eyes
The Maltese Shih Tzu has large eyes but not as protruding as those of the Shih Tzu.

Face
The face is usually shorter than the Maltese but longer than that of the Shih Tzu.

Coat
The Maltese Shih Tzu has a long, thick silky coat.

Living with your Maltese Shih Tzu

Maltese Shih Tzus are said to be happy, playful dogs that adjust to the pace of either an active or sedentary lifestyle. This flexibility makes them good for different age groups.

General behavior
Maltese Shih Tzu owners describe their dogs as friendly, outgoing, curious dogs that like to be with the family.

Activity levels
Maltese Shih Tzus are lively dogs that enjoy regular walks and games. Some Maltese Shih Tzus may like swimming.

Barking
Maltese Shih Tzus will bark like most little dogs, but probably less than the Maltese parent breed.

Temperament
Although the Maltese parent breed can be highly strung and the Shih Tzu calmer and more aloof, Maltese Shih Tzus have a good-natured temperament and are happy to be carried around. If provided with dog toys and chew bones they are not destructive.

The temperament of a dog is directly related to parentage, so discrepancies can exist with any crossbred dog.

Other pets
Maltese Shih Tzus are generally good with other pets.

Children
Maltese Shih Tzus are good with children but, as with all dogs, supervision and training are recommended.

Trainability
Maltese Shih Tzus are bright and easy to train.

Working
Maltese Shih Tzus have been successful as therapy dogs. Their small size and low-shedding coat

may be assets when working with people.

General health and lifespan

The Maltese Shih Tzu is generally a very healthy little dog. The average lifespan for a Maltese Shih Tzu is approximately 12 to 14 years but parent-age is one factor that will influence longevity.

This crossbred may have less problems than the Shih Tzu parent breed because of its longer face, but the eyes of some Maltese Shih Tzus may still be vulnerable to injury or infection. Respiratory problems could still affect some Maltese Shih Tzus, despite the longer snout. Look out for snoring, reverse sneezing, wheezing, or anything to suggest breathing is obstructed.

Watch out for mouth-related problems, as the Maltese parent breed can suffer from mouth diseases as they age if their diet is lacking in hard crunchy food and raw bones. In some cases bite abnormalities could be inherited from the Shih Tzu parent breed.

Other health problems that may affect the Maltese Shih Tzu include skin problems such as itching skin, patellar luxation (a knee problem), hydrocephalus, and liver shunts.

White Shaker Syndrome

White Shaker Syndrome is often seen in the Maltese and occasionally in the Shih Tzu and also in the crossbreds. The cause and the mode of inheritance is unknown. No diagnostic tests are available and the veterinarian will diagnose the condition mostly by clinical recognition. Often the dog will shake uncontrollably and occasionally be unable to walk. White Shaker Syndrome often affects young to middle-aged dogs. To avoid problems, any dogs with this condition should not be used as breeding stock.

Space needs

Maltese Shih Tzus are energetic dogs that do best with a backyard or garden but can live happily in an apartment if they have extra exercise.

Grooming

Maltese Shih Tzus are clean dogs that don't shed a lot of hair. Although low-shedding, the long-coated Maltese Shih Tzu does require daily or weekly brushing and combing to prevent matting. Clipping the dog every three months or so will make grooming easier. The Maltese Shih Tzu is less prone to tear-staining than the Maltese parent breed, but may still require attention.

The Puggle

Name variations: *Pugle, Chinese Begeule, "Miniature Mastiffs"*

Combining two popular small dogs, the Pug and the Beagle, the Puggle has emerged as a crossbred with all-round appeal. The Puggle has a distinctive face, a calm disposition, and a sturdy frame, yet is small enough to live in an apartment. Ideally, the Puggle is less likely to have the breathing problems of the Pug or the bark of the Beagle.

History of the Puggle

The Puggle is one of the success stories of recent attempts at crossbreeding. The Puggle is said to have originated from accidental matings, with the first planned Beagle and Pug crosses taking place in Oklahoma during the 1990s. In a short space of time this healthy, good-natured cross has become one of the United States' leading "designer dogs."

The Puggle's distinctive face resembles the facial appearance of larger dog breeds, yet the Puggle is relatively small. Puggles are sufficiently compact in size to live comfortably in apartments, provided they have regular exercise. This is one reason why the Puggle crossbred has become especially popular in cities like New York.

Recognition of breed

There is no official breed standard for the Puggle. Most Puggle breeders provide first-generation crosses.

Characteristics of the parent breeds

The Beagle parent breed is a small but athletic dog developed over centuries as a scenthound and the Puggle often inherits the stronger physique of the Beagle parent breed.

As a hunting dog, the Beagle has a unique howl that the Puggle is less likely to inherit.

The Pug parent breed is a small, calm companion dog that is admired for its good nature. Unfortunately, the Pug suffers from serious health problems including breathing difficulties that result from its brachycephalic head. The crossbred Puggle usually inherits the elongated snout of the Beagle, reducing the likelihood of breathing problems.

First-generation (F1) Puggles

Puggles are the first-generation cross of a Pug and a Beagle. The Beagle is the dam as the Pug parent breed often has problems whelping. However, care must be taken with the relative sizes of the sire and the dam.

ABOVE First-generation Puggle litter.

Multi-generation Puggles

Puggles have not been developed as a multi-generation crossbred.

Crossbreeding goals

The Puggle has been bred as a small, sturdy, healthy companion dog.

Choosing a breeder

The U.S.-based <www.puggle.org> may help locate reputable Puggle breeders. For Internet searches on the Puggle note that some breeders call the Pug x Jack Russell cross a Puggle (and "Puggle" is also the technical term for a baby Echidna). The most widely known Puggle is the Pug x Beagle cross, so make sure the breeder is providing this particular cross.

ABOVE First-generation adult Puggle with fawn coat and black mask.

A reputable breeder will use good breeding stock and select parents on the basis of temperament as well as looks and genetic soundness. The breeder should also provide proof that the puppy's parents were screened for inherited diseases.

Screening tests

Breeders of Puggles should screen for eye diseases, luxating patellas, hip dysplasia, and Legg-Calvé-Perthes disease. There is currently no genetic test for epilepsy. (See pages 124 to 125 for more information about screening tests.)

Living with your Puggle

Puggles are said to be smart, loving, robust dogs. Ideally, Puggles inherit the good nature of both parent breeds, making them excellent family pets.

General behavior
Puggle owners describe their dogs as sweet tempered, loyal, and affectionate. As with the Beagle parent breed, some Puggles are easily distracted by scents.

Activity levels
Puggles are energetic dogs that love to play games. A brisk daily 30-minute walk helps to keep the Puggle's energy levels down. Puggles also enjoy running and swimming.

Barking
Puggle owners report that the puppies can be barkers and, although less vocal than the Beagle parent breed, some Puggles are prone to howling.

Temperament
Puggles are said to be good-tempered, intelligent dogs with a playful and sociable nature. Puggles tend to be slightly more wary than the Pug parent breed and not quite as trusting as the Pug.

The temperament of a dog is directly related to parentage, so discrepancies can exist with any crossbred dog.

Other pets
Puggles are generally good with other pets.

Children
Puggles are generally good with children but, as with all dogs, supervision and training are recommended.

Trainability
Puggles are fairly easy to train and to teach basic commands. They are eager to please and are said to be good listeners.

Working
Puggles have been used as therapy dogs.

General health and lifespan
The average lifespan for a Puggle is approximately 10 to 15 years but parentage is one factor that will influence longevity.

Puggles that favor the Pug parent breed may have respiratory problems and stenotic nares because of the short face, and associated difficulties such as being susceptible to hot weather and experiencing problems when anesthetized. Although Puggles are less likely to have bulging eyes like those of the Pug parent breed, their large eyes are vulnerable to infection, injury, and problems such as cherry eye (prolapsed third eye).

Other health problems experienced by Puggles may include hypothryoidism, eye problems, skin problems, patellar luxation (a knee problem), hip dysplasia, and Legg-Calvé-Perthes disease (a genetic hip joint disease). Epilepsy is one problem that is inherited in Beagles but it is less likely to be passed on to a Puggle.

Other popular Beagle crosses

Beagle x Basset Hound	Bagel
Beagle x Bearded Collie	Beacol
Beagle x Bichon Frise	Glechon
Beagle x Boston Terrier	Boglen Terrier
Beagle x Boxer	Bogle
Beagle x Cocker Spaniel	Bocker
Beagle x Dachshund	Doxle
Beagle x Golden Retriever	Beago
Beagle x Jack Russell Terrier	Jack-A-Bee
Beagle x Labrador Retriever	Labbe
Beagle x Pekingese	Peagle

VET'S ADVICE

Teeth abnormalities
When choosing a Puggle, look out for malocclusions with the teeth or any other dental abnormality. Many dental problems may not arise until the dog has its full set of teeth.

Mast cell tumors are common in the Pug so a Puggle would also be at risk. All lumps detected should be examined by a veterinarian.

Space needs
Puggles are small enough to be raised in apartments, but they are energetic dogs. Apartment living works best with owners who are home a lot and can take the Puggle on daily walks.

Grooming
Both parent breeds are shedders so be prepared for a dog that sheds. Puggles have a double coat that will probably need weekly brushing and combing as well as regular trimming.

The Beagalier

Name variations: *Beaglier*

The Beagalier is a dog with lots of character and energy. It also has the attractive features of the two parent breeds, the Beagle and the Cavalier King Charles Spaniel. Bred for health and good temperament, the Beagalier is steadily acquiring a following.

History of the Beagalier

The Beagalier became particularly popular through crossbreeding programs in Australia during the 1990s and is still one of the crosses produced by major breeders. Apart from capitalizing on the existing affection for the Cavalier King Charles Spaniel and the Beagle parent breeds, the breeders were looking for a healthy, energetic small dog with a less active scent drive than that of the Beagle.

Recognition of breed

There is no official breed standard for the Beagalier. Most Beagalier breeders provide first-generation crosses.

Characteristics of the parent breeds

The highly regarded King Charles Spaniel has always been a companion dog. Temperament governed selection, leading to several hundred years of breeding for a sweet, nonaggressive disposition. The Cavalier variety, recognized in the 1940s, is popular as a parent breed for its looks and calm temperament and the Beagalier benefits from these qualities.

The Beagle parent breed was developed for a very different purpose, as a scenthound, depending on its nose and stamina to hunt game. It evolved as a good-natured, easygoing pack dog, selected to have no aggression toward other dogs and small enough to be carried by hunters. The popularity of Beagles as working hunting dogs means they have a relatively wide gene pool and no particular structural problems. However, in the modern world, the drive to hunt scent is not necessarily desirable and the Beagle is a notorious wanderer. The Beagalier cross is intended to retain many fine Beagle characteristics but reduce the scent-hunting drive through the Cavalier King Charles Spaniel parent breed, which has no hunting instinct.

The Cavalier King Charles Spaniel has some health problems, including lethal heart conditions and various difficulties caused by its shortened face. Crossing with the Beagle and its longer snout should result in fewer difficulties for the Beagalier.

ABOVE First generation Beagalier puppy with gold markings.

First-generation (F1) Beagaliers

Beagaliers are the first-generation cross of a Cavalier King Charles Spaniel and a Beagle. Either breed can be the sire or the dam as the parent breeds are of a similar size.

Multi-generation Beagaliers

Beagaliers have not been developed as a multi-generation crossbred.

Crossbreeding goals

The Beagalier is interesting as it was primarlly developed to correct a behavioral problem, the scent-hunting drive, rather than for appearance. The Beagalier has been bred as an active, healthy dog that makes a robust family pet.

Choosing a breeder

You may be able to locate reputable Beagalier breeders by asking breeders of other Beagle crossbreds.

ABOVE First-generation adult Beagalier featuring tricolor markings.

A reputable breeder will use good breeding stock and select parents on the basis of temperament as well as looks and genetic soundness. The breeder should also provide proof that the puppy's parents were screened for inherited diseases.

Screening tests

Breeding dogs should be checked by a veterinarian to ensure that they have normal knees and eyes and do not have a heart murmur (which could signify mitral valve disease). X-rays to ensure that hip dysplasia is not present might also be expected, although it is not common in either breed. Breeders should also screen for eye diseases, and luxating patellas. There is currently no genetic test for epilepsy. (See pages 124 to 125 for more information about screening tests.)

Appearance

Beagalier characteristics

There is no official breed standard for the Beagalier. The following are characteristics of a first-generation Beagalier.

General appearance

Beagaliers usually resemble the Beagle parent breed, but with a lighter frame and more puppylike face.

Tail

The Beagalier tail is held from horizontal to about 45 degrees ("gay carriage"). The tail should not curl over the back as this would be a fault in both parent breeds.

Size ranges

A standard Beagalier's height would be approximately 15 inches (38 cm). The mature weight would be approximately 22 pounds (10 kg).

Colors

The Beagalier usually has the black, white, or tricolor coat of the Beagle. The most common of these, "tricolor," is dominant to the red color in "blenheim" or "ruby" Cavaliers and so most Beagaliers are tricolor. If a lemon Beagle is a parent, the puppies will be shades of gold and white. If a ruby Cavalier is a parent, the puppies may be solid-gold colored.

Eyes
The eyes are rounder and more prominent than the eyes of a Beagle.

Ears
The ears of the Beagalier are longer than those of the Beagle.

Face
The Beagalier face is usually shorter than the Beagle face and the head more dome-shaped.

Coat
The Beagalier has a smooth coat, which has longer outer or guard hairs than a typical Beagle. Both parent breeds are shedders, so the Beagalier will probably shed too.

Legs
The legs of the Beagalier are in proportion with its body so it retains "normal" dog proportions.

Living with your Beagalier

Beagaliers are said to have a happy, nonaggressive nature. They make an excellent family dog for people who want a short-haired, robust, and energetic children's pet.

General behavior
Beagalier owners describe their dogs as sweet tempered, friendly, loyal, and reliable.

Activity levels
Beagaliers are lively dogs that benefit from lots of exercise and games.

Barking
Beagalier owners report that the puppies can be barkers but are not yappy dogs.

Temperament
Both parent breeds have good temperaments so the Beagalier is usually calm and good natured. Owners report that the Beagalier usually has a reduced scent-following drive but some, like the Beagle parent breed, can be distracted by scents.

The temperament of a dog is directly related to parentage, so discrepancies can exist with any crossbred dog.

Other pets
Beagaliers are generally good with other pets.

Children
Beagaliers are good with children but, as with all dogs, supervision and training are recommended.

Trainability
Beagaliers are moderately easy to train.

Working
Beagaliers are a relatively new crossbred so they have not yet been tested as working dogs.

General health and lifespan
The average lifespan for the fairly new Beagalier crossbred

is estimated at about 14 years. Parentage is one factor that will influence longevity.

Beagaliers may be at some risk of the lethal heart conditions that affect the Cavalier. The Cavalier parent breed's shortened face may result in soft palate problems, and protruding eyes, which may lead to cherry eye and excessive tear-staining, but these are less evident in the longer-faced Beagalier. Other health problems experienced by Beagaliers may include eye problems, skin problems, patellar luxation (a knee problem), and hip dysplasia.

Heart disease

The Cavalier King Charles Spaniel is prone to mitral valve disease (MVD), where the left AV valve in the heart (which regulates the blood flow in the left side of the heart) is affected. Over time this can lead to congestive heart failure and death. Some dogs with minor to moderate heart disease may live for years with appropriate medication. The average age to develop MVD is approximately three years and older. Reputable Beagalier breeders will ensure that the Cavalier parent dog has been checked by a cardiologist and use only healthy dogs (over 2.5 years with parents older than five years of age and heart-defect free) to reduce the incidence of MVD in the crossbred offspring.

Epilepsy is one problem that is inherited in Beagles but it is less likely to be passed on to a Beagalier.

Space needs
Beagaliers are energetic dogs that do best with an average-sized backyard or garden.

Grooming
The Cavalier has a long shedding coat while the Beagle has a short shedding coat, so be prepared for a dog that sheds. Beagaliers have a short coat that is hairier than the coat of the Beagle. They don't require grooming except for occasional washing (if they get very dirty or smelly).

Other popular Cavalier King Charles Spaniel crosses

Cavalier King Charles Spaniel x Pug	Pugalier
Cavalier King Charles Spaniel x Cocker Spaniel	Cockalier
Cavalier King Charles Spaniel x Lhasa Apso	Lhasalier
Cavalier King Charles Spaniel x Maltese	Maltalier/Cav-A-Malt
Cavalier King Charles Spaniel x Poodle	Cavoodle/Cavapoo
Cavalier King Charles Spaniel x Shih Tzu	Cava-Tzu

The Cavachon

Name variations: *Cavashon*

The Cavachon is a sweet-faced cross between the Cavalier King Charles Spaniel and the Bichon Frise. Many Bichon Frise crosses are sought after for their low-shedding, low-dander coats and the Cavachon is one of the most popular examples.

History of the Cavachon

The Cavachon is highly regarded for its personality, looks, and coat. When used as a parent breed, the Bichon Frise (like the Poodle) can produce crossbred offspring with a low-shedding, low-dander coat that is potentially good for allergy sufferers. The Cavachon is the result of relatively recent attempts to develop Bichon Frise crosses but has gone on to become a very popular crossbred dog (Source: American Canine Hybrid Club survey).

The Cavachon's appeal also lies in the qualities inherited from the Cavalier King Charles Spaniel parent breed, such as a sweet, friendly temperament and varied coat color.

Recognition of breed

There is no official breed standard for the Cavachon. Most breeders provide first generation crosses.

Characteristics of the parent breeds

The Bichon Frise is a popular lapdog brought to Europe in the fourteenth century (and probably originating from Poodle and Maltese stock itself). It has a good-tempered and playful nature. The Cavalier King Charles

Spaniel also evolved as a lapdog prized for its sweet and friendly temperament, so the Cavachon cross makes for a companion dog with a great disposition.

The Bichon Frise parent breed has a distinctive coat with a velvety texture and "powder puff" appearance. The undercoat is soft and dense and the outer coat is of a coarser, curlier texture. However, this low-shedding, low-dander coat does require constant care. The Cavalier King Charles Spaniel parent breed has a moderate length silky coat with a wave but no curl and some feathering on the ears, chest, legs, tail, and feet. The Cavachon offspring usually have full, soft silky coats somewhere between those of the two parent breeds.

ABOVE First-generation Cavachon puppy with tricolor coat.

The Bichon Frise is a white dog with some shadings of buff, cream, or apricot around the ears or on the body. The coloring of the Cavalier King Charles Spaniel parent breed is more varied, including white with rich chesnut markings, and a white blaze. Distinctive color patterns may include buff or copper masks and markings.

First-generation (F1) Cavachons

Cavachons are the first-generation cross of a Bichon Frise and a Cavalier King Charles Spaniel. Either breed can be the dam.

Multi-generation Cavachons

Cavachons have not yet been widely developed as a multi-generation crossbred but in the United States a Cavachon club has been formed with the goal of setting a standard and planning a breeding program (see the American Canine Hybrid Club's Web site). Second-generation Cavachons have less consistency than the first-generation dogs and fewer of the benefits of hybridization.

Crossbreeding goals

The Cavachon has been bred as a small, healthy, great-tempered companion dog. The low-shedding, low-dander coat makes this cross potentially useful for allergy sufferers.

Choosing a breeder

Locate reputable Cavachon breeders by asking breeders of other Bichon Frise crossbreds.

A reputable breeder will use good breeding stock and select parents on the basis of temperament as well as looks and genetic soundness. The breeder should also provide proof that the puppy's parents were screened for inherited diseases.

ABOVE Adult first-generation Cavachon featuring sable coat.

Screening tests

Cavachon breeders should screen for luxating patellas, eye diseases, and heart murmurs. (See pages 124 to 125 for more information about screening tests.)

Other popular Bichon Frise crosses

Bichon Frise x Beagle	Glechon
Bichon Frise x Chihuahua	Chi-Chon
Bichon Frise x Cocker Spaniel	Cock-A-Chon
Bichon Frise x Havanese	Havachon
Bichon Frise x Maltese	Maltichon
Bichon Frise x Pekingese	Peke-A-Chon
Bichon Frise x Poodle	Poochon
Bichon Frise x Shih Tzu	Zuchon
Bichon Frise x Silky Terrier	Silkchon
Bichon Frise x Yorkshire Terrier	Yo-Chon

Appearance

Cavachon characteristics

There is no official breed standard for the Cavachon. The following are characteristics of a first-generation Cavachon.

General appearance

Cavachons usually appear as a combination of both parent breeds.

Tail

The Cavachon tail develops a plume of hair as the dog matures. The tail can be straight, bent, or curled.

Size ranges

A standard Cavachon's height to shoulder ranges from about 11 to 18 inches (28 to 46 cm). The mature weight can be anywhere between 9 and 27 pounds (4 and 12.2 kg).

Colors

Cavachon colors include sable, sable and white, peach, peach and white, apricot and white, lemon and white, red and white, black and white, black and tan, and tricolored. Distinctive color patterns may include buff or copper masks and markings (the "thumbprint" of the King Charles Spaniel is occasionally evident in some Cavachons). Owners report that sable puppies change to white and peach or white and tan as they mature.

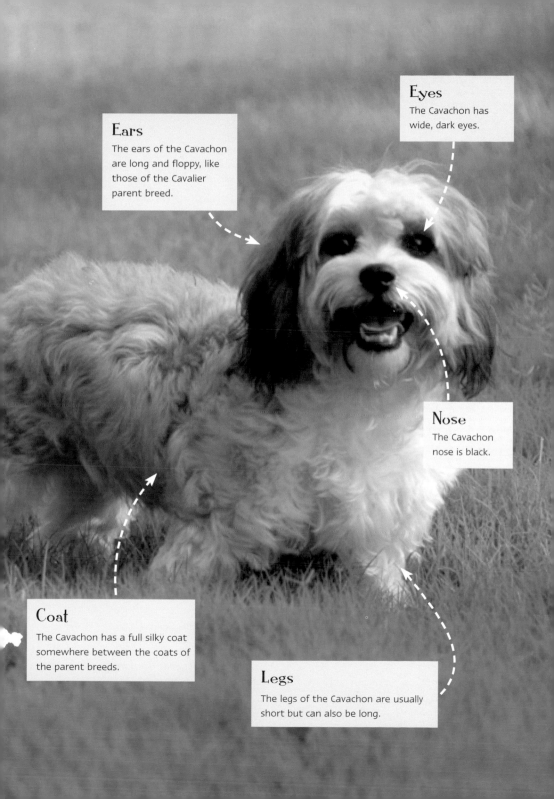

Eyes
The Cavachon has wide, dark eyes.

Ears
The ears of the Cavachon are long and floppy, like those of the Cavalier parent breed.

Nose
The Cavachon nose is black.

Coat
The Cavachon has a full silky coat somewhere between the coats of the parent breeds.

Legs
The legs of the Cavachon are usually short but can also be long.

Living with your Cavachon

Cavachons are said to be loving, friendly dogs that are playful and good with both children and the elderly.

General behavior
Cavachons are described as sweet-tempered dogs with a warm personality that love interacting with the family.

Activity levels
Cavachons need a moderate amount of exercise and will enjoy fetching games. They are playful and some love the water. Owners report that Cavachons display a catlike interest in chasing things, or pouncing and pawing at toys. They are prone to the "Bichon Blitz," running around in bursts of amazing speed and agility for minutes at a time.

Barking
Cavachons are not yappy and, for a small dog, their bark is relatively low-pitched.

Temperament
Both parent breeds are intelligent, affectionate, and nonaggressive, and the Cavachon inherits these qualities.

The temperament of a dog is directly related to parentage, so discrepancies can exist with any crossbred dog.

Other pets
Cavachons are generally good with other pets.

Children
Cavachons are good with children but, as with all dogs, supervision and training are recommended.

Trainability

Cavachons are intelligent and easy to train, but may take a while to house-train as they take longer to mature.

Working

Cavachons have been used as therapy dogs.

General health and lifespan

Cavachons are generally healthy dogs. The average lifespan for a Cavachon is about 10 to 12 years but parentage is one factor that will influence longevity.

Mitral valve disease (MVD) sometimes affects the Cavalier

Eye disorders

Both Cavachon parent breeds, the Cavalier King Charles Spaniel and the Bichon Frise, are prone to certain diseases of the retina (the layer at the back of the eye responsible for detecting light and color), corneal diseases, and cataracts, where the lens loses its nutrition and becomes opaque. A reputable breeder will avoid using breeding stock with eye problems. Owners should monitor any problem-related signs their Cavachon may be showing, including: a bluish tinge to the eye; photophobia (reacting badly to light); subtle signs such as difficulty visualizing distant objects, often in poor light; knocking into "new" objects in the house; being "startled" when touched unannounced; a discoloration/ redness around the eye; pawing or discomfort around the eye; closing the eye; or continually squinting. Owners should talk to their vet to arrange a consultation if concerned.

King Charles Spaniel parent breed but it is less likely to affect the first-generation Cavachon. Reputable breeders will use only healthy breeding stock (over two-and-a-half years whose parents are older than five years of age and are heart-defect free) to help reduce the incidence of MVD in the Cavachon offspring.

Cavachons may suffer from eye problems such as a retinopathy or juvenile cataracts that affect the Bichon Frise parent breed. Other health problems experienced by Cavachons could include patellar luxation and White Shaker Syndrome.

Space needs

With regular exercise, Cavachons can live in an apartment. Owners report that they also do well as outdoor dogs.

Grooming

Cavachons have a low-shedding, low-dander wavy coat that has a silky texture. They are high-maintenance dogs that need to be bathed, brushed, clipped, and groomed regularly. Some second-generation Cavachons may inherit a more Poodle-like coat that needs more clipping.

Selecting your dog

Before you select a breeder or a puppy, do your homework on the crossbred. Seek opinions from veterinarians or dog trainers who are in a position to observe a wide variety of dogs without having a vested interest in one particular crossbred or purebred. Find out about the appearance and temperament of the adult dog. All puppies look adorable and appealing, but puppyhood is brief and you will spend many years with the adult dog.

Are you ready for a puppy? Consider the following questions:

- Is the dog going to be too big/small/boisterous/quiet for your home?
- Have you considered potential health problems?
- Have you considered the cost of vacation care or veterinary treatments?
- Is the current family situation likely to change in the future?

Finding a breeder

If you can offer a good home and know the kind of crossbred dog that would be suitable, start looking for a breeder. It may be difficult to locate reputable breeders of crossbred dogs through Internet searches. Contact local veterinarians or dog trainers, or ask reputable breeders of well-known crossbreds. Purebred dog breeders are unlikely to provide information on breeders of crossbreds.

A reputable breeder will provide proof that the puppies' parents were screened for inherited diseases. Some crossbred puppies are very expensive but high price alone does not guarantee quality. Beware of unauthorized breeders selling what they claim to be a popular crossbred but without evidence of the puppy's parentage. Do not buy dogs from "puppy mills" or from markets and shops that operate as outlets for puppy mills. Puppy mills are substandard kennels where dogs are farmed haphazardly with little regard for health and well-being, for quick commercial gain.

Reputable breeders often have long waiting lists. Use this time to plan for your impending new arrival—agree upon training methods, book a puppy school, shop for the puppy, find the best dog parks, and get the house, fences, and gardens in proper order.

Selecting a puppy from a breeder

Before choosing from a litter of puppies from a breeder you should do your research and prepare questions to ask the breeder, including questions on recent events such as appetite, vomiting, or diarrhea.

At the breeders, take note of the cleanliness and design of the facilities, and how the puppies are reared, exercised, and socialized. Look for a clean, hygienic environment.

The puppies should be in good condition with a good weight, clean ears and eyes, and an excellent coat. Observe the behavior of the puppies. Are you looking for a quiet dog or one that is energetic and boisterous? Occasionally, these characteristics are apparent in a young puppy, though this is not always the case. Be wary of any puppy or young dog that is growling, barking excessively, snapping, biting, jumping excessively, or rushing with bared teeth.

Top ten crossbreds

According to a recent American Canine Hybrid Club survey, these are currently the ten most popular crosses in the United States. Most of the following crosses have been covered in this book; for information on the Shih-Poo, Poochon, and Lhasa-Poo Poodle crosses contact the American Canine Hybrid Club.

Shih-Poo (Shih Tzu x Poodle)

Labradoodle (Labrador Retriever x Poodle)

Cock-A-Poo (Cocker Spaniel x Poodle)

Cavachon (Cavalier King Charles Spaniel x Bichon Frise)

Puggle (Beagle x Pug)

Peke-A-Poo (Pekingese x Poodle)

Poochon (Bichon Frise x Poodle)

Goldendoodle (Golden Retriever x Poodle)

Yorkie-Poo (Yorkshire Terrier x Poodle)

Lhasa-Poo (Lhasa Apso x Poodle)

Be equally wary of a puppy that seems excessively shy and fearful.

Find out about the health and nutrition of the new puppy. Ask a veterinarian if you are unsure. The puppy should be checked by a veterinarian at the vaccine time and given a (documented) clean bill of health.

Answer the breeder's questions and submit an application form. The breeder will have observed how the puppies interact and assessed each puppy's personality and aptitude for different tasks. The breeder takes this information into account when judging the compatibility of a puppy and a prospective owner.

Selecting an adult dog from an animal shelter

Many animal shelters and dog rescue groups have accidentally bred crossbred dogs that are suitable for re-homing (see page 125). Unfortunately, as deliberately bred crossbreds have become popular, many have been abandoned and wound up in shelters. You can do some of the searching for an adopted crossbred online. Breed clubs often provide re-homing services and these may include crossbreds. In the United States different Web sites provide links to dogs in local shelters.

When you choose an adult dog from an animal shelter (or from its "foster family") you will not have the same guarantees that you would expect when selecting a breeder's puppy, such as knowing the breed, temperament, and genetic health of the parent dogs. Information on the dog's recent upbringing (for example, whether it was socialized with children and other pets) may not be available. On the other hand, you may be saving the life of a dog rather than contributing to consumer demands for new dogs that add to the world dog population.

In some respects, selecting an adult dog is easier than selecting a puppy because you already know its mature size, coat type, color, and appearance. As with going to a breeder, you need to observe the dog in its surroundings. Be prepared to ask lots of questions about the breed and mature size of the dog, hygiene, vaccines, worming, de-sexing, exercise, and socialization.

Temperament is one of the main issues when choosing a dog from a shelter. Ask for the temperament assessment of the dog you are looking at. Consider whether the temperament of the dog will fit in with your needs. The dog's previous history (if known) should be communicated. Do not adopt a dog with a known aggression problem.

Before you can adopt a dog, be prepared to be interviewed. Considerations may include children and other family members, where you live, the size of your backyard, the hours that you work, lifestyle, exercise and fitness, illnesses or allergies, and previous experience with animals.

Many institutions advise a settling-in period in the new environment to ensure all is satisfactory. Take it slowly and allow your dog to settle in to its new life.

CHECKLIST: CHOOSING A REPUTABLE BREEDER

☐ **Does the breeder health test the breeding dogs?**

Crossbreds are no more disposed to health problems than the breeds they are comprised of. Hybrid Vigor can produce a positive outcome, but crossbreds are only as disease-free as the actual dogs they were bred from.

☐ **What, if any, health guarantee does the breeder offer?**

Does the breeder stand behind his dogs? How long is the guarantee for?

Most genetic problems will not present themselves within the first year, so a one-year guarantee is not very comprehensive. The guarantee should not be contingent upon you returning the dog, as no one should be expected to return a puppy/dog that is a part of their family. Of course, a breeder cannot be expected to guarantee a dog against every hereditary problem, so most guarantee against all life-altering genetic defects. This would include those hereditary defects that compromise the dog's life to such a degree that it will either have to be operated on, go blind, or will have to be euthanized.

☐ **Why is the breeder breeding dogs?**

What are the breeder's priorities? Is it his dogs, the puppies, selling pet puppies, selling breeding dogs, or his bank statement?

☐ **What is the health schedule for your puppy?**

You should be informed of recommended future treatments and the timing. Worming should have been done from two weeks, on a regular schedule. You should receive a veterinary certificate for the puppy's initial vaccinations. Your puppy's ears should have been cleaned on a regular basis and it should not arrive with an ear infection. Your puppy should not arrive with fleas or flea bites. Your puppy should arrive in good shape with a clean bottom, hair between eyes trimmed so it can see (if a longer-coated dog), and with a pleasant puppy odor, but do allow for accidents during travel to your home.

Does the breeder keep proper records of the breeding program?

Do you receive a pedigree? Does the breeder belong to a breed association and uphold a code of ethics? If so, is your dog eligible for registration? Does the breeder DNA the breeding dogs so inconsistencies can be proven?

Does the breeder provide written care information prior to, or upon, arrival of your new puppy?

Have you been given information regarding what the puppy has been eating?

Are the puppies well socialized?

Does the breeder allow puppies to go at too early an age? Do the puppies receive adequate human contact? Have the puppies spent time in the house?

Does the breeder allow visits to his establishment?

Many breeders will schedule open days so they are not overwhelmed with constant visitors and may have rules for being in contact with young puppies. Do not be offended if you are asked to walk through a footbath, cover your shoes, or remove your shoes, as puppies must be protected from disease, which could be transported on the soles of your shoes. What is the nature of the dogs? What are the conditions like? How much space do the dogs have and do they get regular exercise? What are the dogs fed and do they look like they are in good condition?

For how long does the breeder offer support?

Is it for days, months, or years?

Does the breeder offer referrals that you can actually check?

Do you find the breeder is honest and straightforward?

Are you comfortable communicating with the breeder and getting reasonable responses to your questions?

Does the breeder inform you not only of the positives of owning a dog, but the negatives as well? The breeder should be more concerned that the new owner will be comfortable with the nuisances and any bad habits of the dog than the positives.

The prospective new owner needs to be aware of what to expect, and needs to be well matched to the puppy, so they are both happy in their new living arrangement.

Does the breeder seem knowledgeable and willing to share information or find the answer to a question if he doesn't know it?

Does he have some knowledge of genetics and breed for the improvement of the breed, not the number of puppies he can produce?

Are you screened as to your ability to be a responsible pet owner?

Application forms are not meant to be intrusive, but a useful tool in bringing up some issues you might not have considered.

Caring for your dog

Caring for a puppy

The minimum age for a puppy to leave his mother is between 8 and 14 weeks old, depending on the type of dog and on recommended guidelines. The breeder may also ask for an agreement regarding the age at which a puppy is de-sexed, unless it is being purchased for breeding purposes. Consult your veterinarian before a decision about de-sexing is made. The breeder should also supply details of the puppy's diet so that you can continue the diet and the feeding schedule. The breeder's veterinarian should provide a vaccination card indicating when the next vaccination is due. See the checklist at right for information on caring for your puppy when he arrives home.

Caring for an older dog

Animals age about five to eight times faster than humans. A large 10-year-old Labradoodle may not seem old but it is about the equivalent of a 75-year-old person. Like us, as animals age many things change, so monitor the health and comfort of your dog (see the list on page 122). Avoid startling or waking your dog up suddenly. Avoid exercise on very hot days and provide adequate shade and water. Soft, clean bedding is important. Ensure that your dog has easy outdoor access for toileting. Take your dog for at least annual checkups and if your older dog has an ongoing disease see the veterinarian regularly, as the older dog's health can change very quickly.

CHECKLIST: CARING FOR YOUR PUPPY

Diet

☐ Give the puppy purified water for the first few days so he can gradually adapt to changes in the tap water.

☐ Never instantly change your puppy's food unless instructed by your veterinarian.

☐ Never feed a puppy cooked bones, fish bones, chocolate, onion family items, salt, corn cobs, or egg whites, as these are harmful to dogs.

Health

☐ Do not expose your puppy to other dogs or areas that dogs may frequent until 10 days after he has received his final immunization (at around 12 to 16 weeks of age). Keep your puppy in his crate or on your lap when visiting veterinarians.

☐ Worming should have commenced so check when the puppy is due for worming treatment. Speak to your veterinarian before giving your dog heartworm medication.

☐ Consult the breeder and your local veterinarian about the health issues for your particular crossbred.

☐ Like babies, puppies need uninterrupted naps during the day or they get tired and cranky.

☐ Do not overexercise young dogs, especially the large or fast-growing crossbreds.

☐ Avoid letting puppies, especially the larger, fast-growing, or long-backed crossbreds, climb up and down steps in their first year, as growing puppy hips may not be prepared for the wear and tear that stairs can cause.

☐ A good-quality large-breed puppy food may help when growing spurts start.

Bathing and grooming

☐ If your puppy needs a bath when he arrives at your home use a mild puppy soap recommended by your veterinarian.

☐ Frequent bathing can actually ruin a dog's coat as it already contains natural oils that help repel dirt and water and soaps may destroy these protective oils.

☐ Grooming requirements vary depending on the coat type and this may be difficult to predict in crossbred dogs, as some have a coat change from puppy to adult at any time between 6 and 14 months of age. Their old coat must be groomed out or it will cause severe matting in the new coat.

☐ Consult the breeder and your local veterinarian about the cleaning and grooming issues for your particular crossbred. These might include plucking hair in the ear canal, trimming hair near the eyes, and cleaning eyes, ears, and skin folds on a regular basis.

Training

☐ Before you start training, take the time to consider, as a family, what the "rules of the house" will be for your dog. These should be the rules for the next 15 years or so.

☐ Consistency is the key element of any training goal you might have for your dog, including house-training, leash-training, or basic commands. You must be constant with your training and what you allow and don't allow. Avoid changing "the rules."

☐ As the new pack leader you have to reinforce the pack rules taught by the mother dog and ensure that the puppy is submissive to you, his leader.

☐ Consult the breeder and your local veterinarian about appropriate training strategies for your dog.

☐ Only one person should be in charge of your puppy's training. Multiple trainers will cause your puppy confusion.

☐ Keep your words and requests short and to the point. When giving your dog commands, try and keep the same tone and voice inflection every time the command is made.

Try to use a deeper, soothing quiet inflection, as an excited and higher inflection is a sign of excitement to your dog.

☐ Always keep a loose lead and walk with your dog on the same side when leash-training.

☐ Ignoring a command is a habit that you want to avoid as it is very hard to undo.

☐ Your puppy should never be allowed to "mouth" or "nip" at any time.

☐ Crate training may help with general puppy training, but dogs will need to be introduced correctly to a crate or carrier of the right size and design.

☐ Ten minutes of training daily is better than longer sessions off and on. Your dog will look forward to learning, practicing, and working for you.

Socialization

☐ From an early age puppies seek approval and acceptance, trying to please within their pack and within their home and family. Puppies need to understand that they are at the bottom of the household hierarchy, so they should be subordinate to children and other members of the household.

☐ Supervision and training are necessary when introducing children to the dog. Many smaller dogs will require protection from younger children. Ask your veterinarian for advice.

☐ Check with a veterinarian or dog trainer before introducing the dog to another dog, or introducing it to other animals.

CHANGES IN THE OLDER DOG

- Dietary requirements change so older dogs require different amounts of protein, carbohydrates, and fats. "Senior" diets often take care of these requirements.

- The older dog's appetite may decrease and he may drink slightly more with age, though sometimes the older dog will drink less.

- Coat changes are common with age; sometimes this is due to the effects of UV radiation.

- Dogs tend to need less exercise and sleep more.

- Dogs will often lose muscle mass and "shrink" considerably.

- Barking habits and behavior can change, especially if the dog is unwell or arthritic. Do not leave your dog unsupervised with children.

- Lumps and bumps commonly arise so seek a veterinarian's opinion as the risk of cancer increases with age.

- Very old dogs often show signs of forgetfulness with family members or toileting, which can progress to "doggy Alzheimer's" in certain individuals.

- Most of the body systems change. Common ailments include arthritis, dental disease, heart disease, cognitive dysfunction (behavioral changes due to age), kidney disease, and thyroid disease. Watch out for excessive urination, significant weight gain or loss, coughing or breathing irregularities, difficulty eating or smelly breath, behavioral changes and reluctance to move, morning stiffness, or lameness.

- The dog's sight may be reduced (especially in poor light), so be extra careful in parks and on roads. Hearing is often reduced and older dogs are not as nimble at avoiding trouble.

Recommended reading list

These resources will provide a good introduction to caring for your dog.

Benjamin, Carol Lea. *The Chosen Puppy: How to Select and Raise a Great Puppy from an Animal Shelter*. New York: Howell Book House, 1990.

Coile, D. Caroline. *Encyclopedia of Dog Breeds*, 2nd Edition. Hauppauge, New York: Barron's Educational Series, Inc., 2005.

Dog Owner's Guide Web site: www.canismajor.com/dog

Dunbar, Ian. *Before & After Getting Your Puppy: The Positive Approach to Raising a Happy, Healthy & Well-Behaved Dog*. California: New World Library, 2004.

Fogle, Bruce. *The New Encyclopedia of The Dog*. New York: DK Adult, 2000.

Gough, Alex, and Alison Thomas. *Breed Predispositions to Disease in Dogs and Cats*. Oxford, UK: Blackwell Publishing, 2004.

Kilcommons, Brian, and Sarah Wilson. *Childproofing Your Dog: A Complete Guide to Preparing Your Dog for the Children in Your Life*. New York: Warner Books, 1994.

Kilcommons, Brian, and Sarah Wilson. *Metrodog: A Guide to Raising Your Dog in the City*. New York: Warner Books, 2001.

Padgett, George A. *Control of Canine Genetic Diseases*. New York: Howell Book House, 1998.

Rutherford, Clarice, and David H. Neil. *How to Raise a Puppy You Can Live With*, 4th Edition. Loveland, Colorado: Alpine Publications, 2005.

Volhard, Jack and Wendy. *The Canine Good Citizen: Every Dog Can Be One*. New York: Howell Book House, 1997.

Weisbord, Merrily, and Kim Kachanoff. *Dogs With Jobs: Working Dogs Around the World*. New York: Pocket Books, 2000.

Wood, Deborah. *Help for your Shy Dog*. New York: Howell Book House, 1999.

Appendix: Diseases, health checks and screening tests

DISEASES IN CROSSBRED DOGS

Crossbred dogs can get the same diseases as purebred dogs. Some of the main diseases are mentioned in the breed profiles and are described as follows.

Cushings disease: An endocrine (hormonal based) disease where the adrenal gland, which is positioned near the kidney, becomes overactive and produces excessive amounts of "steroid" hormones.

Diabetes: A disease caused by a deficiency in insulin, a hormone produced by a special part of the pancreas. The pancreas sits in a loop of the small intestine and is a very complicated fragile organ. Diabetes can occur at any age but is most commonly seen in dogs over six or seven years (though a rare form is possible in puppies). Typical signs are drinking, eating and urinating excessively, lethargy, and vomiting. In dogs, most of the cases of diabetes require insulin injections and dietary changes to control the signs and keep the glucose levels in the body as stable as possible.

Elbow Dysplasia (ED): A disease of unknown cause, although like HD, it is thought to be a combination of genetic and environmental predisposing factors. It is the abnormal development of certain areas of the canine elbow during the dog's "growth phase." These changes may often lead to elbow arthritis. Initial signs include sudden or gradual forelimb lameness, and pain and stiffness, especially after rest or on cold mornings.

Epilepsy and seizures: Epilepsy refers to the (possibly inherited) condition that leads to seizures that occur for unknown reasons. A seizure is a muscular response to an abnormal "firing off" of nerve signals from the brain. We often refer to seizures as mild (or localized)—"Petit Mal"—to severe (and generalized)—"Grand Mal." Seizures may also be caused by toxins, metabolic or electrolyte imbalance, infectious diseases, and neoplastic (cancerous) disease, for example. These are sometimes referred to as "secondary epilepsy."

Hip Dysplasia (HD): An abnormality in the development of the hip joint. It is a very complex disease characterized by genetic and environmental predisposing factors. The "socket" or acetabulum is often very shallow and the "ball" or femoral head undergoes a remodeling process due to increased joint laxity. The result is often lameness, a "waddling" gait, exercise intolerance, pain, and restricted movement when manipulated.

It is complex because (1) Dogs appear to be born with normal hips and develop the disease with time. (2) Many dogs with HD do not exhibit the above signs. (3) Full radiographic signs often do not develop until the dog is fully grown (up to 18 months or two years in certain breeds). Therefore, the signs can "change" with time. (4) Besides genetic predisposition, many environmental factors may be involved. Contributing factors include rapid growth and weight gain and overexercising in young dogs.

Hypothyroidism: The result of an underactive thyroid gland producing inadequate amounts of the thyroid hormone, thyroxine. The gland is located in the neck and its main function is to control the body's metabolism. The disease is often seen in older dogs and may lead to weight gain, skin diseases, hair loss, mental depression, and inactivity.

Legg-Calvé-Perthes disease: A disease of the hip joint that has an inherited component. The part of the top of the hind limb that articulates with the pelvis loses its nutritional blood supply and dies off for unknown reasons. This disease is common in certain Toy breeds.

Liver shunts: An abnormality of the vessels where blood is diverted from the abdominal circulation to the heart (away from the liver), which means the liver does not get to remove the toxins from the blood. Shunts can be congenital or acquired and be present (in single or multiple form) inside or outside the liver. Toy breeds can be affected as well as some other breeds such as Schnauzers.

Otitis: Often an infectious or allergenic inflammation (or thickening) of the ear canals due to infectious bacteria or yeasts or the effects of allergic ear disease (for example, from a food allergy or atopy).

Patellar Luxation: A congenital (present at birth) and inherited condition of the stifle (knee), although it can also be caused by trauma later on in life. It is a dislocation (luxation) of the kneecap (patella) that can lead to pain, lameness, stiffness, and eventually cause severe arthritic changes. Toy or small breeds are more prone to medial patellar luxation (except when it is caused by trauma) than other large breeds.

Progressive Retinal Atrophy (PRA): A hereditary disorder of the retina (located at the back of the eye, this tissue layer contains rods and cones, which are involved with night and day vision respectively). Common initial signs include a dilated pupil(s), night blindness, increased reflectivity and cloudiness of the eye. This often progresses to complete blindness. Commonly affected breeds include Poodles, Cocker Spaniels, and Labradors. Different types of Progressive Retinal Atrophy (PRA) are caused by different genes; for example it can be recessive in one breed and dominant in another. PRAs in one breed may not be the same as PRAs in another breed.

Von Willebrand's disease: The most common inherited bleeding disorder in dogs. Affected dogs have a reduction or absence of von Willebrand's factor, a blood protein involved in binding platelets (part of the blood primarily involved with the clotting process) to blood vessels. This disease can be life threatening due to the possibility of uncontrolled bleeding. Many breeds are predisposed including the German Shepherd Dog.

HEALTH CHECKS AND SCREENING TESTS

Many conditions can be identified and avoided if the breeder has screened the parent dogs for inherited diseases and the crossbred offspring has regular health checks at the vet. Different types of tests are listed below.

DNA tests: DNA profiling is becoming more popular with breeders and dog owners. Potential puppy purchasers can ask if DNA health status certificates will be supplied by the breeder. A parentage verification system is used to confirm the identity of a puppy's parents (dogs have been known to jump

fences!) and ensure that the owner gets what he is paying for. Color checks test for recessive colors. This helps the breeder predict the colors of a litter. As many puppies are "booked" by prospective owners well in advance of their birth, DNA color typing can provide more information before a litter arrives.

DNA testing can check for some genetic diseases, such as prcd-PRA, or identify which dogs are clear or carry dominant PRA (see Eye tests). DNA testing labs also provide long-term archiving of DNA samples so breed clubs can keep records on the development of dogs like the Australian Labradoodle.

Eye tests: Many inherited eye disorders can be tested by a skilled practitioner or specialist. DNA testing can also help with eye diseases. DNA testing for prcd-PRA is now being used to help avoid one form of Progressive Retinal Atrophy (PRA). Another test on the dominant form of PRA gives breeders the information required to exclude affected dogs from further breeding. CERF (The Canine Eye Registration Foundation) is a U.S.-based foundation where ophthalmologists can identify eye diseases and register them. This helps breeders and ophthalmologists track eye diseases. Examinations are conducted annually so diseases that appear later in life, such as PRA, can be monitored.

Elbow Dysplasia tests: Screening for elbow dysplasia is carried out via a clinical examination and radiography by the veterinarian then sending radiographs to an elbow dysplasia accredited scheme.

Hip Dysplasia (HD) tests: All dogs are subject to hip dysplasia (HD) but some breeds are more prone to it than others. Dogs may be x-rayed before the age of two but as they may still be growing most breeders wait until after the dog's second birthday.

Any veterinarian can take X-rays of a dog's hips but some are more experienced or accredited in different screening processes. The Orthopedic Foundation for Animals (OFA) is a U.S. certifying body for hip and elbow dysplasia, and other genetic canine diseases. OFA has a database that shows the hip and elbow evaluations for thousands of dogs www.offa.org. Dogs that are registered with OFA certifications can be verified online by putting in the dam or stud's registered name, registration number, or OFA number. The consumer is encouraged to ask the breeder for the OFA information so the consumer can verify it online. A qualified veterinarian can take an OFA radiograph for submission to OFA for hip and elbow evaluation.

The University of Pennsylvania Hip Improvement Program (PennHIP) is a radiographic technology (X-ray) for hip evaluation. PennHIP also holds a large scientific database that is used for learning more about canine hip dysplasia (CHD). More information is available at <www.pennhip.org>.

Even if parent dogs have been cleared this does not mean their offspring is free from hip dysplasia. Hip dysplasia can skip generations or only affect one single puppy.

The best approach is to view the problem in terms of probabilities: the larger the proportion of the dog's close relatives that do not show HD, the greater is the chance that the animal will not get HD, and will not produce offspring with HD.

Luxating Patella tests: A veterinarian can screen for luxating patellas via a physical examination.

Skin tests: Most dogs start to develop allergies only from 18 months of age onward. Blood tests and intradermal skin tests are used to test the current state of the dog.

Temperament tests: Breeders may conduct temperament tests (such as the *Puppy Aptitude Test*, developed by Joachim and Wendy Volhard) on puppies between six and twelve weeks of age. Testing can give general ideas about behavioral traits, and whether the puppy's disposition matches what the prospective owner wants. However, puppies may change in their responses to these tests over time, or if they are ill. The best guide to temperament is the temperament of the parents.

Useful contacts

Crossbred dog organizations

Labradoodles
The Australian Labradoodle Association (ALA)
Web site: <www.laa.org.au>
Australian Labradoodle Association of America (ALAA)
Web site: <www.ilainc.com/USAClubs.html>
The International Australian Labradoodle Association (IALA)
Web site: <www.ilainc.com>

Cockapoos/Spoodles
Cockapoo Club of America
Web site: <www.cockapooclub.com>

Goldendoodles
Goldendoodles.com
Web site: <www.goldendoodles.com>

Yorkiepoos
Yorkiepoo.org
Web site: <www.yorkiepoo.org>

Maltepoos
North American Maltipoo/Maltepoo Club and Registry
Web site: <www.maltipooclub.com>

Puggles
Puggle.org
Web site: <www.puggle.org>

General
American Canine Hybrid Club
Web site: <www.achclub.com>

Animal welfare organizations

USA
American Society for the Prevention of Cruelty to Animals (ASPCA)
424 E. 92nd Street
New York, NY 10128-6804
Phone: (212) 876 7700
Web site: <www.aspca.org>

CANADA
The Canadian Society for the Prevention of Cruelty to Animals (CSPCA)
5215 Jean-Talon O
Montreal, PQ, H4P 1X4
Phone: (514) 735 2711
Web site: <www.spca.com>

AUSTRALIA
Royal Society for the Prevention of Cruelty to Animals (RSPCA) Australia Inc
PO Box 265
Deakin West, ACT 2600
Phone: (02) 6282 8300
Web site: <www.rspca.org.au>

Animal Welfare League
1605 Elizabeth Drive
Kemps Creek NSW 2178
Phone: (02) 9826 1555
Web site: <www.animalwelfareleague.com.au>

UNITED KINGDOM
Royal Society for the Prevention of Cruelty to Animals (RSPCA)
Wilberforce Way, Southwater, Horsham, West Sussex RH13 9RS
Phone: (0870) 33 35 999
Web site: <www.rspca.org.uk>

Blue Cross
Shilton Road, Burford, Oxon OX18 4PF
Phone: 01993 822651
Web site: <www.bluecross.org.uk>

NEW ZEALAND
Royal New Zealand Society for the Prevention of Cruelty to Animals (RNZSPCA)
PO Box 15349
New Lynn, Auckland
Phone: (09) 827 6094
Web site: <www.rspcanz.org.nz>

Index

Photo credits

PAGE 2: Carrie Allen. **PAGE 5:** James Young/James Young Photography.

INTRODUCTION: Page 7 Jack Phipps/Black Dog Photography; all other photos James Young.

EXPLANATION OF TERMS: Page 12 Guide Dogs Queensland; all other photos James Young.

CHAPTER 1: Page 20 (top) Melinda Radus/Sunset Hills Labradoodles; page 20 (bottom) Kathy Young/Cloudcatcher Labradoodles; page 21 used with permission of Royal Guide Dogs Association of Australia; page 22 (left) James Young; page 22 (right) Kathy Young; page 23 Melinda Radus; page 24 (inset) Melinda Radus; pages 24–25 Kathy Young; page 26 (left) James Young; page 26 (top right), Melinda Radus; page 26 (bottom right) James Young; page 27 Kathy Young; page 28 (left) Kathy Young; page 28 (right) James Young; page 29 (top) Melinda Radus; page 29 (coat types) Melinda Radus.

CHAPTER 2: Page 30 (bottom) Marg Laughlin/Rivergum Designer Puppies; all other photos Guide Dogs Queensland.

CHAPTER 3: All photos James Young.

CHAPTER 4: All photos James Young.

CHAPTER 5: Page 52 (top) James Young; page 52 (bottom) Marg Laughlin/Rivergum Designer Puppies; page 53 James Young; page 54 (left) Michael Barry; page 54 (top right) Carole Schatz; page 54 (bottom right) James Young; page 55 James Young; page 56 (inset) Marg Laughlin; pages 56–57 James Young; page 58 (left) James Young; page 58 (top right) James Young; page 58 (bottom right) Marg Laughlin; page 59 (left) Amy Lane, Fox Creek Farm; page 59 (right) James Young.

CHAPTER 6: Page 60 (top) Malinda DeVincenzi/Darby Park Doodles; page 60 (bottom) James Young; page 61 JC Puppy; page 62 (inset) James Young; pages 62–63; Malinda DeVincenzi; page 64 (left) Malinda DeVincenzi; page 64 (right) Malinda DeVincenzi; page 65 (top left) Malinda DeVincenzi; page 65 (bottom left) Malinda DeVincenzi.

CHAPTER 7: Page 66 (top) Jack Phipps/Black Dog Photography; page 66 (bottom) Shannon Woodrow/Shannon's Shamrock Kennels; page 67 David Wolfe; page 68 (inset) Robin Cahill; pages 68–69 Jack Phipps; page 70 Jack Phipps; page 71 (left) Lynda Kadziorski; page 71 (right) Jack Phipps.

CHAPTER 8: Page 72 (top) Mary Jane Kovacs, Doodle Treasures; page 72 (bottom) Kristine Robards/Double R Aussies; page 73 Laura Fenton; page 74 (inset) Kristine Robards; pages 74–75 Daryl Woods; page 76 (left) Kristine Robards; page 76 (right) Tracy Pozayt/Rebelsrun Kennels; page 77 (left) Tracy Pozayt; page 77 (right) Tracy Pozayt; page 78 (left) Laura Fenton; page 78 (right) Kristine Robards; page 79 (left) Monica Capobianco; page 79 (right) Daryl Woods.

CHAPTER 9: All photos Heather Hill/www.yorkiepoo.org

CHAPTER 10: Page 86 (top) James Young; page 86 (bottom) Bronwyn Hinder; page 87, James Young; page 88 (inset) Margaret Hennessy/Dogue; pages 88–89 James Young; page 90 (left) James Young; page 90 (right) Steven Scott/Country Puppies; page 91 James Young.

CHAPTER 11: Page 92 (bottom) Steven Scott/Country Puppies; all other photos James Young.

CHAPTER 12: All photos Chelle Calbert/Chelle Calbert Photography.

CHAPTER 13: Page 106 (bottom), Sarah Levy; all other photos James Young.

CHAPTER 14: page 110 (top) Kelly Teaff; page 110 (bottom); Cindy Kintzel/Cavachon Connection; page 111 Carrie Allen; page 112 (inset) Linda Rogers/Timshell farm; pages 112–113 Carrie Allen; page 114 (left) Cindy Kintzel; page 114 (right) Sandy Wasicek, Rosegate Kennels; page 115 Carrie Allen.

CHAPTER 15: Page 117 (Labradoodle, Goldendoodle, Cockapoo, Pekapoo) James Young, (Puggle) JC Puppy, (Yorkiepoo) Heather Hill, (Shih-poo) Penny Rangi, (Cavachon) Cindy Kintzel, (Poochon) Vanessa Jordanovich, (Lhasa-Poo) Matthew & Sara Manuel/www.lhasapoo.org; page 119 Melinda Radus.

CHAPTER 16: All photos James Young.

Acknowledgments

The responsibility for the text rests solely with the authors of the text. The following advisers are gratefully acknowledged for their assistance with this book:

Frank Nicholas, ReproGen; Kate Schoeffel, www.familypets.com.au; Velma Violet Harris, Velma's Pets as Therapy; Melinda Radus, Sunset Hills Labradoodles; Kathy Young, Cloudcatcher Labradoodles; Guide Dogs Victoria; Dianna Cooper, Australian Support Dogs Inc NSW; Lauren Elgie, Guide Dogs Queensland; Gwen Gillespie, Southeastern Guide Dogs Inc.; Sonja Walsh; Josie Montanari, Cockapoo Club of America; Amy Lane, Fox Creek Farm; Michelle Dinwiddie, Piney Mountain Puppies; Malinda DeVincenzi, Darby Park Doodles; Shelley Rodes, PeaPods Pekapoos; Garry Garner, American Hybrid Club; Joy Parkin, Shady Maple Doodles; Marcy Lilly, High Lonesome Ranch; Shannon Woodrow, Shannon's Shamrock Kennels; Tracy Pozayt, www.rebelsrun.net; Kris Robards, Double R Ranch and Kennel; Mary Jane Kovacs, Doodle Treasures; Heather Hill, www.yorkiepoo.org; Marg Laughlin/Rivergum Designer Puppies; Chelle Calbert, www.designerdoggies.com; Samantha Howell, Snuggles Puggles; Linda Rogers, Timshelll farm; Teresa Hulvey; Sandy Wasicek, Rosegate Kennel.